Dancing With Daddy

Knowing the Father Intimately, The Desire of a Holy Bride

By

Sheila Mangum

ACW PRESS
ACW Press
5501 N. 7th Ave. #502
Phoenix, AZ 85013

Dancing With Daddy

Cover design by Eric Walljasper
Cover illustration by Michael Hansen
Page design by Steven R. Laube

Printed in the United States of America
ISBN 1-892525-21-6

Dedication

This book is dedicated to my Heavenly Father for answering a prayer
To my Heavenly Bridegroom for bringing it to the Father on my behalf
To my mother for praying it

Acknowledgments

Steve, the love of my life, thank you for taking such good care of me. I will forever be in awe of your love for me.

Mom, thanks for the many hours of prayers you continually lifted up! He *is* the God of all joy and all comfort! You were right!

Boo, thank you for the many laughs you have given to me to press on! I could never have hand picked such an amazing sister.

Lee Ann, my spiritual sister, thank you for the "kisses" and "Q-tips" from Daddy! I can see our Jesus all over you! Thank you for all you have done for this book!

Dr. Joe Brown and Teresa, my spiritual parents, thank you for believing in the Jesus in me.

Jack and Linda, only Jesus could adequately thank the two of you. And He will. I pray for all of your dreams to come true.

Irene, our hearts are knitted together forever. Jesus is building our rooms beside each other right now! I love you!

Angela, Susan, Vicki, Lori, Stephanie and April, my faithful friends, thank you for taking such good care of my family and me. I couldn't have written this book without your love and confidence to strengthen me every day. I love you all deeply!

Joan, my songbird, you are my present from God for writing this book for Him. I love your song, but most of all I love your heart.

Brittany and Stevie, I love you both and so does Jesus!

Contents

Introduction

My Dear Friend,

I am so thankful that you are here for a journey with me. God has sovereignly placed this book in your hands. My prayer for you has been that you become more intimate with your Heavenly Father and pursue His desire for your life! You are the daughter of the Creator of the universe! There is a very high calling for your life and you are to walk in a manner that is worthy. You are to live as a child of God so that you can prepare yourself to be the bride of Christ.

I must tell you that when God laid on my heart His dream for writing a book I couldn't believe the call was for me. The more that I get to know God, the more astonished I am that I am His vessel. I take great comfort in the fact that He spoke through a donkey!

He revealed to me that I was to be His pencil one day during a song and a trip to the library. He outlined the chapters to include such topics as grace, love, mercy, fatherhood, weddings, suffering, and spiritual warfare. It seemed like such a perfect book. At first I was on a cloud writing away five chapters. To me my life was close to perfect. Then things changed. How? I was called to live and relive *all* the chapters. Writing the last chapters became a life changing time.

Notice that I mentioned chapters on suffering and spiritual warfare. I can tell you truthfully that Satan was allowed to attack me as hard as I could physically and mentally stand. (I am thankful for the scripture that says God will never give you more than you can handle!) You will never see the tears that have been poured over these pages. You will never know how much strength God had to give me to endure. You will never feel the ache of the broken heart that stayed with me for months.

What I hope you will feel, after reading this book, is an intimacy with God. I can honestly say that I have been as close to God as I could ever dream to be. What will this book teach you (other than the only way to get tears out of a computer keyboard is with a Q-tip)?

It will teach you to run to the *all* powerful, *all* comforting arms of God and *dance away*. It will teach you to walk in the freedom and power purchased for you at Calvary. It will teach you to endure with all your heart the journey laid out in order for you to attain your eternal inheritance. It will teach you how to prepare for the return of your Heavenly Bridegroom by becoming more like Him. It will teach you that no one loves you like your Heavenly Father and you are to rest intimately in that love.

This book will change your life. It has changed mine. I am grateful to be His vessel "For Such a Time as This." If you listen to the truths revealed in this book and live them you will be dancing straight toward the arms of the One who loves you completely! You will become all that you were called to be from before the creation of the world. That is exciting isn't it? Are you ready? Let's go!

Dance On!
Sheila

Chapter One

My Promise

The Lord is faithful to all his promises
and loving toward all he has made. (Psalm 145:13)

When my little Brittany says to me, "Do you promise, Mommy? A promise is a promise!" I pay close attention. I always try to keep my promises to her. In fact, if she really wants to make sure that I am going to do what her heart is asking, she has me do the "pinkie promise!" That means the promise is serious business! My mind is then set on her promise and I do all I can to follow through.

Why is this so important to me? I have found that the most amazing part of my life came from a promise. It was a promise that my father made to me. This promise was made to me before I was born.

Sadly, I never knew of this promise for more than twenty years. Once I found out about the promise my life was never the same. I never knew promises were so full of love and trust until I experienced one for myself. I should say that it was a kept promise that inspired me. My father had told someone of this promise and together they wrote it down for me to have when I needed it. Let me explain myself:

Here Comes the Bride!

You see, it all started with my wedding. A wedding is a busy exciting time, and the rush of it can be overwhelming. The big day had finally come, yet something was wrong. Yes, I was marrying the man of my dreams! It was the day of my dreams! All around me were my most special friends and my loving family, amidst spring flowers and a gentle breeze. Sound perfect? Yes, it does! Except for one thing: you cannot see someone's pain inside. There was something missing and I felt it deeply. I felt this something missing had to be found before we could go on. I went searching for the problem. I peeked through a side door and saw my handsome uncles seating people for the wedding. I was touched by the fact that they were there for us. I shut the door and smiled. My heart immediately sank. It was then that I realized that what was missing. It was my father.

Four years earlier my father had committed suicide. I had loved him dearly. The reality of something like this happening to a person is indescribable. The pain took over my insides. It spread like cancer. I felt deserted, lonely and unworthy of love. People can always blame themselves. I was forever thinking of it. It changed my whole being. I felt as though his death left me with a different heart than I was born with. I felt like a completely different person. I can still see that little girl in my mind to this day. I started to find things I didn't like about myself that I had never noticed before. I felt unsure and insecure. My father had left us. Why would he do that? What did I do wrong? What was happening to me? There was only one thing that I knew for sure and that was that I had to hide this pain.

The first few years after his death took a great toll on me. I had done a tremendous job "band-aiding" the pain, but an even more successful job in my hiding the pain from others. I had to portray an image of worthiness even though I did not feel it. I felt that if people knew the real me they would reject me as well. Fear and rejection are bondage to the soul. My soul could not breathe, for the pain overtook it. How could I set my soul free? I felt it crying for help. I needed to find that answer. It consumed me.

Plans had been made for my brother to walk me down the aisle. I was really fine with that. But what I was missing most at that moment was the presence of my father. I needed him to *smile* at me, to *encourage* me, to *laugh* with me, to *love* me, to *watch* me, to *listen* to me, to *hug* me, and to *dance with me*. There would be no special father-daughter dance at my wedding and it was painfully obvious to me.

I was so happy with my future husband Steve, I needed to tell my dad all about it. I needed to hear back from him, " I love him, too. He's great! I know that he will take good care of you! I am so proud of you both! You look beautiful today! I will always be there if you two need me!" But he had never even met my husband.

On a bride's wedding day she is around all the people in the world who love her devotedly. I was "one minute from hugging distance " from all of them. I knew that if I shared with anyone in that church that my hurt was tremendous, he or she would have responded in love. My future husband would have worried all day. My mother would have cried. My sister's heart would have bled. The sanctuary would have been full of tears. Still, I knew that there was nothing that anyone could do. So, I kept my pain to myself. It was the happiest day of my life, yet pain was in my heart.

Pain, Pain Go Away!

I had always hidden my pain. Do you know the pain I am talking about? It's the heaviness in your heart that only goes away when you are asleep. Then you wake up (because that is a part of sleeping, otherwise you might opt not to wake up). You're up and an unusual feeling comes upon you. It feels good. Then you search your brain for an answer to what's going on! You feel good! This is a strange feeling! You start to wake up and you are thinking, who am I? What am I doing? Where am I? Eventually, you will find that memory file that reminds you of who you are. Also, that you live with a heaviness in your heart. You aren't supposed to feel happy. It takes maybe a good whole three minutes after you have awakened, then the pain is back. The sad part is that this "sleeping roller coaster" happens to you every day. Sometimes more than once a day if your pain has you sleeping a lot.

It is the pain that people try to avoid. People try to fill this particular void with many different things such as money, religion, alcohol, drugs, other people, food, or material things. That is what I was doing in my life when something happened; something that I had never dreamed could happen; something that filled the emptiness in my broken heart; something that cured my soul; something that changed me into another person. This is when I found out about my promise.

A Promise is a Promise!

I found my promise in Psalm 146 verse 9. *The LORD watches over the alien and sustains the fatherless and the widow.* My mother once told me that God would provide special people throughout my life to take the place of my father at the times I needed them. She continued to explain to me that God knows what we need and that He will take care of us, just as He does the birds in the trees because He loves us. It sounded very encouraging for someone else, but that could not be for me. I didn't feel loved. No one could love me. She assured me it was true.

Would God care enough about me to sustain me? I cried out for His help! I felt foolish. God had to be too busy with others to send someone to help me. It never really registered that He might answer my cry. I was acting out of emptiness and still feeling unworthy to be asking for His help. I was fully content or so I thought with the fact that one day I would go to heaven because I believed that Jesus was the Son of God. But while I was on earth the pain that happened to be given to me by "life" would just have to be. But what did that promise mean? *I will sustain the fatherless.* I was so sure that it felt unreal I left my promise behind. I went looking in all directions for my cure. I had forgotten all about my promise.

God did not forget that promise! Soon I realized that God did hear my cry. It was so amazing to me. I could hardly contain my joy. I was fully aware that all that was happening to me was straight from Him. I never wanted this unbelievable feeling to go away. That feeling has never left me. It's a feeling of security, of acceptance of love, hope, peace and joy. Those are such common words, but few people actually receive them. I felt blessed!

He did arrange in the heavenlies for someone to fill that emptiness. He did send someone to *smile* at me, to *encourage* me, to *laugh* with me, to *love* me, to *watch* me, to *listen* to me, to *hug* me and to *dance* with me. God had provided for me what He had promised in His Word: a father to the fatherless. You are asking yourself, " Who did He send? A godly neighbor? A special Pastor?" God sent...*Himself.*

What Pain?

His name is the LORD-and rejoice before him.
A father to the fatherless, a defender of widows,
is God in his holy dwelling. (Psalm 68:4b-5)

My life has changed. When I wake up in the morning, a very special feeling comes upon me. It feels great! I search my brain for an answer to what's going on. I ask myself, "Who am I?" The answer...*God's child.* "What am I doing?" *Glorifying Him.* "Where am I?" *In His arms.* Knowing that my life is in the hands of a sovereign, loving, holy God who has made me for Himself is the start of a glorious day. I am safe. I am loved. I am secure. I am in *His presence.* More than that I am in His lap talking to my Daddy. What a safe place to be!

Dancing with Daddy

You turned my wailing into dancing; you removed my sackcloth and clothed me with joy, that my heart may sing to you and not be silent. O LORD my God, I will give you thanks forever.(Psalm 30:11)

There is a wedding at which my Father will be. His presence will be known. His love will be surrounding the place. This joy will be eternal. After the Marriage Supper to the Lamb, I will be dancing with my Daddy. I will take the hand that created me. *(Colossians 1:16)* I will hold the palm that has my name written on it. *(Isaiah 49:16*) I will dance on His feet and let Him guide just as he has all my life. *(Psalm 23:3)* I will look into the eyes that have watched me. *(Psalm 145:20)* I will dance in the arms that I have run to so many times. *(Proverbs 18:10)* I will reach out and touch the face of love. *(Psalm 31:16)* I will be with Him for eternity. This will be the happiest day of my life without any pain in my heart. The best part of it all is that this will be a familiar time for my Father and me because this is our relationship now. It's a bond that existed even before the wedding, before the kingdom, before the new Jerusalem, before the new heaven and new earth. It's a bond that you can have today. He has been faithful to reveal Himself to me. He has loved me completely and I have felt it. I look forward to that day. So does He. *Do you?*

God's Desire for You

This book is for you. It is His desire for you to understand who you are in Christ Jesus to your heavenly Father. You are part of Him. You are His child. You are the love of His life. Your security is that He loves you! He wants you to know of your relationship with Him so that when you are in heaven you can confidently take your position as Christ's Bride. You are joint heir to all that is His. *(Romans 8:17)* God has plans for your life. Plans of good and joyous things. *(Psalms 68:3)* He wants your life to be full. *(John 10:10)* He loves you so much that He cannot take His eyes off of you. It's true!

It is my prayer that you know Him, really know Him. I pray for you to know that he answers the lowliest of prayers like mine. I pray that you will know that He created you and chose you to be His own. He loves you unconditionally and made all provisions for you to receive His love. He planned to love you before the creation of the world *(Ephesians 1:4)* and He is thinking of you right now.

You will never know God fully until you know Him as Father. We can know God the Father through Jesus the Son. *Because you are sons, God sent the Spirit of his Son into our hearts, the Spirit who calls out, "Abba, Father. So you are no longer a slave, but a son; and since you are no longer a slave, but a son; and since you are a son, God has made you also an heir.* (Galatians 4:6-7) "Abba" in this scripture actually means Daddy! You can call Him Daddy! I love what Max Lucado says, "If God had a wallet your picture would be in it!" God loves you so much that He would move the sun one-inch to shine on your face to feel His love. As you read this book, it is my prayer for you to have eyes only for Him and listen to what promises He has for you.

To conquer the pain of this world you have to have an accurate belief about yourself based on what the word of God says! Our personal histories shape and mold our insides. Our personal relationship with the Father comforts and transforms our insides. *He heals the brokenhearted and binds up their wounds.* (Psalm 147:3) Do you have a broken heart? Do you fear tomorrow? Are you unsure of your future? The word of God tells us that you are a child of the King and bride of the King of Kings. Are you ready to confidently take your position as Christ's bride? Are you excited about knowing the Father intimately? *Don't you think it's time you took a dance with Daddy? Let's begin!*

Chapter One Study Questions

Before you begin pray for the wisdom and discernment needed to study His Holy Word!

Write out and read aloud Colossians 1:16.

all things were created by God.

Who created you? Why did He create you?

God To glorify Him.

Write out and read aloud Isaiah 49:16

He inscribed me on the palms of His hand.

Does God have to tie a string around His finger to remember you or is He forever mindful of you?

No

Write out and read aloud Psalm 23:1-3

The Lord is my Shepherd. I shall not want, He leads me beside still waters. He restores my soul. He leads me to green pastures.

Who takes care of you?

God

Who can restore your soul?

God

Where will God always guide you?

beside still waters

Will you follow?

Yes

Read 2 Chronicles 16:9 to find out what the LORD does for those who are fully committed to him? WOW!

He shows Himself.

Write out and read aloud Proverbs 18:10.

The name of the Lord is a strong tower where we are safe

What happens to the righteous when they run to the LORD?

We are safe.

Read Romans 3:10 to find out who is righteous enough to fellowship with God?

None

Read Romans 3:22-24 to see how someone can become righteous?

by believing in Jesus

Read aloud Ephesians 2:8-9 and fill in the blanks:

For it is by grace you have been saved, through faith - and this is not from yourselves, it is the gift of God – not by works, so that no one can boast.

What does this verse say the reason is for God not saving us by "good works"?

so that

It is by grace you have been saved, through faith!

Read Ephesians 2:1-2 and find out what condition we are in without saving grace through our Lord Jesus.

We were dead in sin.

Write out and read aloud Isaiah 54:10

The mountains & hills shall depart but my kindness will not be removed from you.

What word describes God's love in this verse?

Kindness

Write out and read aloud Matthew 6:26.

Look at the birds of the air. They dont sow or reap yet the Heavenly Father feeds them.

The little bird is trusting in God's provision, are you? Are you singing as cheerfully as the little birds at God's gift of provision, peace and rest?

Write out and read aloud Ephesians 1:4-5.

He chose us in Him

When were God's first thoughts of you?

He loved us.

How does the symbol of adoption make you feel?

Good.

Write out and read aloud Psalm 68:3.

Let the righteous rejoice before God.

Who does God want to be happy and joyful?

Me

Write out and read aloud John 10:10. The thief comes to steal - Jesus came so that we might have life more abundantly.

What does Jesus promise in this verse?

That we would have life abundantly.

Jesus wants you to have a life full of love, joy, peace, contentment, and freedom. It's a promise my friend! You can count on His promises. Read Psalm 145:13b.

He promises that His kingdom will endure for ALL generation

Write out and read aloud Jeremiah 29:11

For I know the plan I have for you says the Lord.

God has specific plans for your life; what are those plans?

plans for me to prosper

Write out 2 Corinthians 6:18. I will be a father to you & you will be my sons & daughters.

What does God say He will be to you?

a father

What are you referred to in this passage?

his daughter

Write out and read aloud Psalm 30:11. What is wailing/ mourning turned into?

dancing

Are you dancing? Praise God

Close in prayer.

Chapter Two

Daddy's Dreams: A Bride for His Son

I saw the Holy City, the new Jerusalem, coming down out of heaven from God, prepared as a bride beautifully dressed for her husband. Revelation 21:2

A father to the fatherless. Let's take a closer look at that promise. *His name is the LORD-rejoice before him. A father to the fatherless, a defender of widows is God in his holy dwelling Psalm 68:4b-5.* His name is the LORD. LORD here is more than a word. It is a relationship. Who is that relationship with? The Creator of this universe! He is to be Lord of your life. Lord, in all capital letters is translated from the Hebrew word YHWH, Yahweh or Jehovah, meaning the self-existent one. He is the great I AM (Exodus 3:14). He is eternal, the Alpha and the Omega, the beginning and the end (Revelation 1:8). He is the same yesterday, today, and forever. He does not change. He is a covenant-keeping God (1Chronicles 16:15). He will never fail you. He keeps his promises. Are you holding onto his promises? A Christian holds onto God's promises and lives by their guidance and power. Knowing God's promises has shown me life's greatest reward-Him (1 Corinthians 9:24). In order to know Him you must know His promises. His promises are in the Word of God, your Bible. All you need to know about God is in His holy Word. So let's start from the beginning and reveal to you more about your creator, Father.

Our Jewish Roots

God introduced himself personally to the world through the children of Israel. God is the God of the Jewish patriarchs Abraham, Isaac, and Jacob. He is the only true living God. He is also referred to as The Father of Israel. God made a covenant with them through Abraham known as the Old Covenant. In the covenant God promised them land and a seed who eventually came to be known to the world as Jesus Christ the Messiah. Moses and Joshua, descendants of the fathers of Israel eventually led the children of Israel out of slavery to their Promised Land.

During their journey God gave them many laws and customs they were to live by to be righteous in his sight. Every law and custom given was for their own good. God had to reveal to them His holiness and give them direction and guidance in their lives. He set them apart so that He could make Himself known to the rest of the world. We as believers today are also to be set apart so that the world can see God's plan in Jesus. There were many wonderful customs given to the children of Israel that illustrated God's plan for the world. Let's start with the ancient Jewish wedding customs.

Ancient Jewish Wedding Customs

A wedding is the perfect illustration of love. Weddings are always the making of a happy ending. Most of the fairy tales that I read my children end with a wedding and the words, "They lived happily ever after." Weddings are always the same, to join two people to become one. There is the honored bride with radiant beauty. The bridegroom is always wearing a smile that never seems to leave his face. He is so proud of his future wife and this makes her feel like royalty. It is the most special time for two people who are made for each other. God unites them. When two become one in God, marriage becomes a holy sacred union. God introduced to the Jews the sanctification of marriage and then elevated it to a holy relationship. This is where the term "holy matrimony" comes from.

God's heart desire is to prepare a Bride for His Son Jesus. You could say that the Church and Jesus Christ were made for each other! God is preparing the greatest love story ever to be told and you are included. The greatest event of all ages will be the Wedding of the Lamb of God and His Bride. The ancient Jewish wedding ceremony is the perfect illustration of how God is preparing for that day. God gave the Jews specific instructions on marriage. God then revealed to the world that He wanted to put sanctity and order in the marriage relationship. In the pagan world you could "acquire" a wife by just taking her home. Women were not equal in worth to men in this time. God wanted to start his love story by showing love and respect to the bride. Let's look further to see how the bride is chosen.

Choosing the Bride

It was always the father or the bridegroom who pursued the bride-to-be. Let's read John 15:16: *You did not choose me but I chose you and appointed you to go and bear fruit that will last.* God chooses the bride for his Son. What an amazing thought! We have been chosen to be part of Messiah's Bride. We are unworthy, yet we are so loved.

There is an illustration in the Bible of how the father of the bridegroom would send his most trusted servant out to search for the bride. Let's read in Genesis the story of Abraham sending out Eliezer to find a bride for his son Isaac.

> *Abraham was now old and well advanced in years, and the LORD had blessed him in every way. He said to the chief servant in his household, the one in charge of all that he had, 'Put your hand under my thigh. I want you to swear by the LORD, the God of heaven and the God of earth, that you will not get a wife for my son from the daughters of the Canaanites, among whom I am living, but will go to my country and my own relatives and get a wife for my son Isaac.' The servant asked him, 'What if the woman is unwilling to come back with me to this land? Shall I then take your son back to the country you came from?' 'Make sure that you do not take my son back there,' Abraham said. 'The LORD, the God of heaven, who brought me out of my father's household and my native land and who spoke to me and promised me on oath, saying, " To your offspring I will give this land"-he will send his angel before you so that you can get a wife for my son from there. If the woman is unwilling to come back with you, then you will be released from this oath of mine. Only do not take my son back there." So the servant put his hand under the thigh of his master Abraham and swore an oath to him concerning this matter."* (Genesis 24:1-9)

Eliezer then went on his journey looking for Isaac's bride. Eliezer asked the God of Abraham for help. *Then he prayed, 'O LORD, God of my master Abraham, give me success today and show kindness to my master Abraham.'* (Genesis 24:12) This is a wonderful love story! Genesis 24 is a revelation of the heart of God, that His Son would have a bride. We are reaching the very heart of God in these passages.

Who is God's most trusted servant today? He is the Holy Spirit! The Holy Spirit is seeking a bride for God's

Son right now. This servant is working night and day preparing this precious bride for God's Son. Do you remember the time when he came to you? *No eye has seen, no ear has heard, no mind has conceived what God has prepared for those who love him-but God has revealed it to us by his Spirit.* (1 Corinthians 2:9-10)

The Holy Spirit reveals to us who Jesus is, just like Eliezer revealed to Rebecca who Isaac was. (Genesis 24:34-49) We have not yet seen Jesus, but through the Holy Spirit we are becoming more and more acquainted with him. 1 Peter 1:8 says, *Though you have not seen him, you love him: and even though you do not see him now, you believe in him and are filled with an inexpressible and glorious joy, for you are receiving the goal of your faith, the salvation of your souls.* Are you filled with an inexpressible and glorious joy from getting to know our Bridegroom?

Engagement

The word betrothal means engagement. The Hebrew word for betrothal is *erusin*. The betrothal in ancient times was much like our engagement period today. The ancient Jewish engagement was a formal, legal and binding covenant that was more important than the wedding itself. The "engaged" couple was legally married at this point. However, they would not live together for months.

Another word used in the Hebrew language for this part of the ceremony is *kidusin*, which means sanctification. Sanctification is to be holy, with the idea of being set apart. As Christ's bride we are to be holy and set apart from the rest of the world. People will then know that we belong to Jesus. Does the world know that you belong to Jesus? Does His holiness set you apart?

How do we become holy? Holiness comes from yielding to the Holy Spirit. The Holy Spirit and the Holy Word of God helps us to be transformed into the likeness of Jesus. *For those God foreknew he also predestined to be conformed to the likeness of His Son, that he might be the firstborn among many brothers.* (Romans 8:29) In ancient times the bride would spend her time apart from her bridegroom preparing herself for him. How can we do that? Becoming more Christ-like is being a prepared bride. We are to yield to the Spirit and fill ourselves with Him. Jesus then gets a perfectly compatible Bride. Are you preparing yourself for Him?

Obtaining holiness is a life long process. The process is well worth the pain and wait. I have found it painful battling our three enemies: this world, Satan and the flesh. Overcoming ourselves to be filled with the fruit of the Spirit is work, but it is not impossible because we have our Bridegroom to help us. John 16:33 tells us that Jesus has overcome the world! 1 John 4:4 tells us that the Spirit who is in us is greater than the one in the world. Do you believe that? That is a promise my friends. Yielding to the Spirit is the key to opening the door for more of Him.

Because of Him, we are a Bride who is holy, spotless and blameless. We are able to have full fellowship with a holy God because of Jesus. *Husbands, love your wives, just as Christ loved the church and gave himself up for her to make her holy, cleansing her by the washing of the word, and to present her to himself as a radiant church without stain or wrinkle or any other blemish, but holy and blameless.* (Ephesians 5:25-27) How do we become spotless and blameless? It is by the blood of our heavenly Bridegroom and the Holy Word of God.

His blood has cleansed us of all sin. We are then in a holy relationship with God. We have been reconciled back to God. *All this is from God, who has reconciled us to himself through Christ and gave us the ministry of reconciliation: that*

God was reconciling the world to himself in Christ, not counting men's sin against them And he has committed to us the message of reconciliation. (2 Corinthians 5:18-19) Our sins are washed away by the blood of Christ and nothing is held against us.

The Word of God changes our sinful nature and washes us of all that is not Christ-like. I have personally needed to be drowned in the Word of God. I have had a very stubborn, prideful, yet sensitive nature. However, every time I come up for air I am breathing Christ's very life inside me. The feeling is so powerful and refreshing. John tells us in John 3:30, *He must become greater; I must become less!* That's our goal! Less of us, more of Him!

The consecrated or holy bride of Christ is His most treasured possession. *The Lord your God has chosen you out of all the peoples on earth to be His people, his treasured possession.* (Deuteronomy 7:6) We are His treasure. We are His hearts desire. *For where your treasure is, there your heart will be also.* (Matthew 6:21) Jesus is longing for the day to be with you in eternity. You exist to be loved by Him. Well, that is breathtaking! Dunk me again!

Veil

Once engaged the bride would show that she was spoken for by wearing a veil to cover her face. This showed others that she was spoken for and purchased by another. Are you keeping yourself veiled from the temptations of this world by separating yourself from it? Are you spoken for? Have you accepted the engagement of being bought by the blood of Jesus? Are you set apart from the rest of the world by your holy life? Are you keeping yourself pure for your bridegroom? Good questions!

Our House

The betrothal/engagement could last as long as twelve months. Although the couple was considered married, the young man would have to leave to go to his father's house to prepare their bridal chamber, the place where they were to live. This bridal chamber of ancient times was the *huppah*, meaning room or covering. This was a special room built onto the bridegroom's father's home. (Ringing any bells?) Let's read what Jesus said in John 14: 2-3: *In my father's house are many rooms: if it were not so I would have told you. I am going there to prepare a place for you. And if I go and prepare a place for you, I will come back and take you to be with me that you also may be where I am. You know the way to the place where I am going.* Scripture tells us that Jesus has left earth to go and prepare a place for us to live. *I saw the Holy City, the New Jerusalem, coming down out of heaven from God, prepared as a bride beautifully dressed for her husband.* (Revelation 21:2) Could our bridal chamber be the New Jerusalem? Could be!

New Covenant

There was then a marriage contract that was presented to the father of the bride. This was referred to as the *ketubah*. It included what the bridegroom was willing to do to take care of his bride now and in the future. The most important part of this proposal was the "bride's price," or the *mohar*. Brides in ancient Israel were purchased. The *ketubah* consisted of what the young man was willing to pay for his bride. The price was paid to her father. Let's read 1 Peter 1:18-19: *For know that it was not with perishable things such as silver or gold that you were redeemed from the empty way of life handed down to you from your forefathers, but the precious blood of Christ, a lamb without blemish or defect.*

Jesus gave the most valuable thing in the world for you ... Himself. Many times the father of the bridegroom would decide the terms of the marriage contract and the son would carry it out. Do you see how valuable you are? God put together a plan in your marriage contract for you to be purchased and the Son carried it out. He died to purchase us. He rose from the dead to give us pardon from the past. When Jesus died on the cross the "bride price" was paid. *It is finished!* (John 19:30) You belong to Jesus.

We have a marriage contract today that is full of more promises from our Bridegroom: our Bible. This marriage contract is described in the Bible as the New Covenant. Your marriage contract is the Gospel of Jesus Christ. Brides would cherish their *ketubah*. Are you cherishing yours and holding onto every word? He is faithful and true! (Revelation 19:11) Jesus will never leave you at the altar.

It is important to know that even though the Father of the bridegroom would select the bride, her part was to accept willingly. Remember the example of Abraham and Eliezer? In Genesis 24:57-58 it tells us that Rebekah was asked after she was chosen, "*Will you go with this man?" Then they said, "Let's call the girl and ask her about it." So they called Rebekah and asked her, "Will you go with this man? "I will go," she said.*

She had a choice and she accepted. Do you see the picture of free will? God never makes anyone accept his Son. The Holy Spirit will knock and knock and knock. However, we have to respond. We have to choose yes or no to accept Christ. My favorite thing about my marriage is that my husband wants to be with me. It is the "wanting" that makes relationships work. Do you want to be with Jesus? Have you accepted this marriage proposal?

Cup of Wine

In ancient Israel if the marriage contract was acceptable to the father, the young man would then pour a cup of wine to be shared with his bride-to-be. He would wait for her to drink it. This sealed the marriage contract. It showed her acceptance of his marriage proposal. The shared cup represented the new life together. Today, we accept this covenant with the meal of communion. Let's read what Jesus said at the Last Supper with his disciples in Luke 22:19-20: *And he took bread, gave thanks and broke it, and gave it to them, saying, "This is my body given for you; do this in remembrance of me." In the same way after the supper he took the cup saying, "This cup is the new covenant in my blood, which is poured out for you."*

There was a second cup of wine in Jewish customs that would be shared months later at the actual taking home of the bride. Let's read Jesus' referring to this second cup in Matthew 26:29: *I tell you, I will not drink of this fruit of the vine from now until that day when I drink anew with you in my father's kingdom.* You will be present for this cup to be shared. Isn't that a heart stopper! *Come and share your master's happiness!* (Matthew 25:21) Are your feet moving now?

Chapter Two Study Questions

Before you begin pray for the wisdom and discernment needed to study His Holy Word!

Take some time to read Genesis 24 entirely and reflect back on the chapter you just read.

Who did Abraham send to find a bride for his son Isaac?

His servant

Who was the she?

Rebekah

Did Rebekah have a choice? (Genesis 24:57-58)

Yes

Who does God use to search for a bride for His Son? (Romans 8:16-17)

Holy Spirit

Do you remember the time He came to you?

Yes

Review again Eliezer telling Rebekah and her family of Isaac in Genesis 24:34-49. Then read I Corinthians. 2:9-10 and I Peter 1:8.

The Holy Spirit reveals to us Christ Jesus. Let's read Jesus' words before He left earth in John 16:7: *But I tell you the truth: it is good that I am going away, the Counselor will not come to you; but if I go, I will send him to you.*

What is the Holy Spirit called in that verse?
the counselor

In John 16:13 we see what a wonderful counselor from God the Holy Spirit is to us. *"But when he, the Spirit of truth, comes, he will guide you to all truth. He will not speak on his own; only what he hears; and he will tell you what is yet to come."*

He will guide you to ALL truth! What is the truth and what does the truth do for you?
Jesus

If you hold to my teaching, you are really my disciples. Then you will know the truth, and the truth will set you free. John 8:31-32

The truth is the Word of God and it will set you free!

Write out John 8:36: Therefore if the Son makes you free, you will be free indeed.

Read 2 Corinthians 1:21-22 and fill in the blanks:
Now it is God who makes both us and you stand firm in Christ. He sealed us, set His _______ of __________ on us, and put his Spirit in our hearts as a deposit, of what is to come.

The Spirit is just a deposit guaranteeing what is to come. WOW! *How exciting!*

We have learned that Spirit reveals to us who Jesus is. The Spirit pursues us. We make the decision to accept Jesus or not. Once you have accepted Christ as your Lord and Savior you belong to Him. He has purchased you through the blood on the cross as His bride. You are then set apart and called to holiness. Let's read 2 Timothy 1:9 and fill in the blanks:

But join with me in __suffering__ for the __gospel__, by the power of __God__, who has __saved__ us and __called__ us to a __holy__ life-not because of anything we have done but because of His own __purpose__ and __grace__.

Ephesians 5:25-27 tells us two things that can make us a holy bride. What are they? holy
without blemish

The blood of Jesus and the Word of God will wash out every stain, wrinkle and blemish you have. You may be covered with the blood right now. But are you constantly washing yourself with His Holy Word?

Read John 17:17 and fill in the blanks:

Sanctify them with the __truth__; your __word__ is truth.

What four things are the scriptures used for in 2 Timothy 3:16-17?

1. doctrine
2. reproof
3. correction
4. instruction in righteousness

What is the result of obeying God's Word? (verse 17)

We will be complete.

What does obeying God's Word do to your relationship with Christ? (John 14:21)

He will manifest Himself in us.

How does obeying God's Word show outwardly? (1 John 2:5-6) the love of God will be perfected in Him.

Read Hebrews 4:12 and fill in the blanks:

For the __word__ of God is __powerful__ and __sharp__. Sharper than any double-edged sword, it penetrates even to dividing __soul__ and __spirit__, joints and marrow; it __discerns__ the __thoughts__ and __intents__ of the heart.

Close in prayer.

Chapter Three

Wedding of the Century

Let us rejoice and be glad and give him glory!
For the wedding of the lamb has come,
and his bride has made herself ready.
(Revelation 19:7)

It is at the celebration of the engagement that the bridegroom brings gifts for the bride-to-be. This would be so that she would know of his love and be reminded of him while he was gone. She would treasure her gifts and use them to think of him often. Let's look at the gifts that Eliezer gave Rebekah to show Isaac's love in Genesis 24:53 and see how it relates to Christ and the church: *Then the servant brought out gold and silver jewelry and articles of clothing and gave them to Rebekah; he also gave costly gifts to her brother and to her mother.*

He gave her gold, silver, and garments. Gold is symbolic of God's deity. Gold represents Christ living in us. Gold is His nature, it is His life. The streets in heaven are pure gold. (Revelation 21:21). He alone is worthy of such riches. We are to be transformed into his likeness and be of his very nature (2 Corinthians 3:18). He is our gift, how wonderful!

Silver represents redemption; we are redeemed through the blood of Jesus (Ephesians 1:7). Your relationship with God has been restored through the blood of your heavenly Bridegroom as a gift. This gift brings forth a committed grateful heart. Judas betrayed Jesus for thirty silver coins. Silver represents the blood money for redemption and atonement.

The garments represent the work of transformation. We are told in the Bible that we are to be given many garments to wear. We will first wear the garment of salvation and the robe of righteousness. *I delight greatly in the Lord; my soul rejoices in my God. For he has clothed me with garments of salvation and arrayed me in a robe of righteousness, as a bridegroom adorns his head like a priest, and as a bride adorns herself with jewels*. (Isaiah 61:10) Later, we will wear the linen garments representing the righteous acts of the bride. *Let us rejoice and be glad and give him glory! For the wedding of the Lamb has come, and his bride has made herself ready. Fine linen, bright and clean, was given her to wear. Fine linen stands for the righteous acts of the saints.* (Revelation 19:7-8)

The wedding gown of the church will be their righteous acts. This is a difficult verse for us to grasp because we all know that we are not righteous one little bit. How can we stand before our Bridegroom in our own righteousness? We as believers will be judged not for our sins in regard to our salvation. We are already clothed with the garment of salvation. However, we are to be judged for our rewards. (1 Corinthians 3:10-15)

What is our standard to follow? Jesus. Obedience to Jesus is the key. We are to live a life dedicated to His teachings. We are to act on His Word. We are to follow the Holy Spirit's prompting. We are to yield to His Spirit so that he can weave Himself into our lives. He stretches us so that we finally say yes to His will, yes to His desires, and yes to His character. He then weaves Himself into our hearts. When we allow Christ to do His work through us we are weaving our wedding garment. The Holy Spirit is the weaver. We are to put ourselves into His hand and He will prepare us.

Our wedding garment is the work of God. However, the responsibility is our own. We are responsible to let

God weave His Son's life into us. You weave with a needle. Needles can cause pain. It is painful to choose this garment. But, that is how the bride makes herself ready! What are you doing to adorn your wedding gown? What are you doing for the Lord? Remember this, God desires for your rewards to be full! Are you ready to walk down the aisle of righteousness?

Gift of the Spirit

In modern times the bridal gift would be known as an engagement ring. Every bride-to-be cherishes her ring and it is a reminder that she belongs to someone. What gifts has our bridegroom left us to remind us of him? The Holy Spirit is our constant reminder of Him. Through the Holy Spirit we use and enjoy many gifts from the bridegroom. In Galatians we see some of them, *But the fruit of the spirit is love, joy, peace, patience, kindness, goodness, faithfulness, gentleness and self-control. Against such things there is no law.* (Galatians 5:22-23. Other gifts are in Romans 12 and 1 Corinthians 12.)

The Holy Spirit reveals Him to us. There is nothing more valuable than the character of Christ felt in you! What a wonderful gift He has left us. Pray daily for the Spirit to have more control of your life so that you can feel the presence of the Bridegroom. I have the feeling that none of us is using our gifts to the extent Jesus plans for us to. Pray about that!

A New Life with Jesus

Brides in ancient Israel, as well as brides in Israel today take a special bath before their wedding. It is called the *mikveh*. The word *mikveh* means a pool of living water used for ritual purification. It is part of a ceremonial cleansing that prepares her for the days ahead. It represents a separation from an old life to a new life. A new life with her bridegroom is anticipated. In 2 Corinthians 5:17 we see, *Therefore, if anyone is in Christ, he is a new creation; the old has gone, the new has come!*

Our baptism in the New Covenant is our symbolism of a new life today. Colossians 2:11 says, *In him you were also circumcised, in the putting off of the sinful nature, not with a circumcision done by the hands of men but with the circumcision done by Christ, having been buried with him in baptism, and raised with him through your faith in the power of God, who raised him from the dead.* We are a new creation in Christ when we accept him as our Lord and are baptized into a new life with him. You are a new creation in Him. You are His creation.

The *mikveh* represents a change in status and authority for the bride. It represents the bride coming out from the authority of her father and to the authority of her husband. Before accepting Christ, your spiritual father was the Father of Lies, Satan. *You belong to your father, the devil, and you want to carry out your father's desire. He was a murderer from the beginning, not holding to the truth, for there is no truth in him. When he lies, he speaks his narrative language, for he is a liar and the father of lies.* (John 8:44).

When we are one with Christ we are dead to sin and no longer under the authority of Satan. (Galatians 2:20) What is our new status under the authority of Jesus? Read 1 John 3:1: *How great is the love the Father has lavished on us, that we should be children of God! And that is what we are!* Does your marriage contract to Jesus elevate you to the worth of a man? Absolutely not! It puts you on a pedestal. You now have the worth of a King!

The apostle Paul tells us of the change we have in Christ Jesus, *I pray also that the eyes of your heart may be enlightened in order that you may know the hope to which he has called you, the riches of his glorious inheritance in the saints, and his incomparable great power for us who believe.* (Ephesians 1:18-19) Now that is a change in status! You are royalty! *But you are a chosen people, a royal priesthood, a holy nation, a people belonging to God, that you may declare the praises of Him who called you out of darkness into His wonderful light.* (1 Peter 2:9)

The Wedding

The wedding itself would be taking home the bride. When the bridal chamber was complete the decision would come from the bridegroom's father that it was time to get his bride. The bride in ancient Israel would have no idea when the bridegroom would come back to get her. She would not know the date, time or hour. Let's read about this in Matthew 24:36: *No one knows about that day or hour, not even the angels in heaven, nor the Son, but only the Father.* She would have to sleep with what she needed for her new life beside her bed. She would have to be ready for him to come at any minute.

Jewish bridegrooms usually would return for their brides very late in the evening, some time close to the midnight hour. *At midnight the cry rang out: Here's the bridegroom! Come out to meet him!* (Matthew 25:6) The big event would start with a procession in the streets. Shofars (ram's horn) would sound and torches would light the street to follow the bridegroom and his closest friends to his bride.

This will be the climax to the love story that our Heavenly Father is preparing! The Son of God in all His power and glory comes back for His bride sweeps her off her feet and rescues her from this evil world! 1 Thessalonians 4:16-17 says, *"For the Lord himself will come down from heaven, with a loud command, with the voice of the archangel and with the trumpet call of God, and the dead in Christ will rise first.*

After that, we who are still alive and are left will be caught up together with them in the clouds to meet the Lord in the air. And so we will be with the Lord forever." Did you catch that last sentence? We will then be with Him forever. When the bridegroom returned, the bride was ready for him. Are you prepared to leave with Jesus when He returns? Are you ready for forever with Jesus?

Are you fearful of His return or are you joyful? If you love the King of Righteousness you will be anointed with joy and will anticipate His return! Jesus has been anointed with the oil of joy Himself. *You have loved righteousness and hated wickedness; therefore God, your God, has set you above your companions by anointing you with the oil of joy.* (Hebrews 1:9) You were the joy set before him on Calvary! He died for you to be His joyful bride. Now, that will put Joy, Joy, Joy down in your heart!

The Bride Revealed

It was a custom in ancient Israel for the bride to be wearing her veil when she left with the groom. No one in town knew who she was until they returned to town after their wedding. It is when Christ returns to earth to rule and reign as King that the Bride will be with him. Her veil will be lifted. This is when she is revealed to the world. Can you hardly wait until God says to the world, "This is my Son's Bride, whom I love; and with whom I am well pleased"? Can you imagine the smile on Jesus' face? I live for that smile.

Our Celebration

The Ancient Jewish weddings lasted seven days (Genesis 29). The guests began the celebration as the bride and bridegroom would be alone in the bridal chamber. The second cup of wine would be shared and the marriage covenant would be sealed forever! After the marriage was consummated the bride and bridegroom joined their guests for the joyous feast. This will be the Marriage Supper to the Lamb for Christians. This will be the happiest time you and I will ever know. This will be a beautiful time between Christ and His bride (you!).

What will we feast on at this wedding feast? We will be able to feast on His love, compassion, wisdom, knowledge, beauty and strength. We will be eternally united with our Bridegroom. Guess what? We will then be dancing with Daddy! *Let them praise His name with dancing and make music to him with tambourine and harp. Psalm 149:3* Can you hardly wait? It is the day that Jesus is longing for. His perfect heart yearns for you. Let me say that again: *His perfect heart yearns for you!*

Every detail in your life, good and bad is preparing you for Him. While your Bridegroom is away you are to be preparing to be His Bride. There should be nothing that comes between you and the joy of knowing that. Life has been hard for you, I know. Change has come that you have not expected. The joy in your heart seems to have been stolen. Your insides have hurt. I know that pain. I can feel it right now for you. It's awful! Change is difficult to go through. However, God *is* still on the throne and Jesus *is* still at His right hand. The only time that will change is when Jesus returns for you! You should find great comfort in that!

Let me tell you something else you need to know. Jesus feels your pain even more than you do! He is using your life's situations to teach you to dance with Him. Rest on His shoulder! Hold His hand! Kiss His Face! Follow His voice! Your faith in Him will start a sweet song! Sing to the music of His grace and mercy! He sings over YOU! *The LORD your God is with you, he is mighty to save. He will take great delight in you, he will quiet you with His love, he will rejoice over you with singing.* (Zephaniah 3:17) Can you feel the tenderness of His song?

He loves you! He is working day and night interceding to the Father on your behalf. *Christ Jesus, who died-more than that, who was raised to life-is at the right hand of the God and is also interceding for us. Romans 8:34.* His heart's desire is for you to press on toward Him. *I press on toward the prize for which God has called me heavenward in Christ Jesus.* (Philippians 3:14)

Rest in his arms! *The Lord replied, "My presence will go with you, and I will give you rest."* (Exodus 33:14) He will wipe away every tear. *The Sovereign Lord will wipe away the tears from all faces.* (Isaiah 25:8) Are you accepting your invitation to this wedding? *The Spirit and the bride say, "Come!" and let Whoever is thirsty, let him come; and whoever wishes, let him take the free gift of the water of life.* (Revelation 22:17) *Then the angel said to me, "Write: Blessed are those who are invited to the wedding supper to the Lamb!" And he added, "These are the true words of God."* (Revelation 19:9) Can He have this dance?

Your future bridegroom is eagerly awaiting your answer. Or you may have already accepted Him and want to renew your vows. Give Jesus your heart and let Him give you His. He died to give you His heart.

This is one wedding that Daddy doesn't mind paying for! What is the Bride's wedding present from the Father? Eternal Life! John 17:3 tells us that eternal life is knowing Him! What a glorious gift! Dance away!

And they lived eternally ever after!

"Amen. Come, Lord Jesus." Revelation 22:20

Chapter Three Study Questions

Before you begin pray for the wisdom and discernment needed to study His Holy Word!

For what reason did Christ say that He was leaving His disciples? (John 14:2) He left to prepare a place for them.

In John14:3 He tells them something very important. Write out that promise. I will come again to get you so that you can be with me.

What three things will sound when Jesus returns? (I Thessalonians 4:16) a shout
voice of an archangel
trumpet

Will we ever again be separated from Him? (I Thessalonians 4:17) We will always be with the Lord.

What happens to us when we see the Lord? (I John 3:2-3)
We will be like Him.

Read Matthew 25 and find out about the 10 virgins. Which ones went to the wedding?
the ones that were prepared

What happened to the other virgins?
they missed the bridegroom

Read Matthew 22 and find out why the man was thrown out of the Wedding Banquet?
He didn't have on the wedding garment

Read Isaiah 61:10 and fill in the blanks:

I delight greatly in the LORD; my soul rejoices in my God. For He has clothed me with garments of salvation and arrayed me in a robe of righteousness, as a bridegroom adorns his head like a priest, and as a bride adorns herself with jewels.

What garments are available for you?

salvation & righteousness

Write out our wedding announcement from Revelation 19:7-8. Rejoice - the marriage of the Lamb has come.

What does this announcement say about the Bride in verse 7? The Bride has made herself ready.

She made herself ready. How? Let's keep going and we'll discover how!

What kind of clothing did she wear? (Revelation 19:8) What does it represent? fine linen, clean & bright

The righteous acts of the Saints, is the work of the Holy Spirit in our lives. We are to be His yielded vessels in works and in refining.

Read Romans 13:14 for the threads of our wedding garment. The Lord Jesus Christ

The character of Jesus has to be woven in us. Jesus then has the perfectly compatible bride He is waiting for!

Read Revelation 16:15 for an important message from Christ Jesus!

Be ready - keep your garments close.

Read 2 Peter 3:14 for the condition we need to be in when Christ returns.

without spot & blameless

Who knows the day and he hour that Christ will return? (Matt.24:36)

no one

Read 2 Peter 3:13 and fill in the blanks:

But in __________ with his promise we are looking forward to a new heaven and a new ~~heaven~~ earth, the home of the righteous.

How is the new heaven and new earth described here?

a place where righteousness dwells

Read Revelation 22:5. How long will the bride of Jesus reign with Him?

forever

Consider, How long did you plan and prepare for your earthly wedding, which lasted a few hours? Our purpose in life is an eternal purpose. Be prepared for Jesus!

Close in prayer.

Chapter Four

Dressing Like Daddy

My prayer is not that you take them out of the world
but that you protect them from the evil one.
They are not of the world even as I am not of it.
Sanctify them by the truth; your word is truth.
(John 17:15-17)

We have discussed in chapter one the Fatherhood of God and in chapter two and three the Bridegroom of Jesus. Let's talk a little bit about you and your part in this love story. You have been called to be in the family of God. We discussed how the desire of God's heart is to glorify His son Jesus and to bring forth a bride that will be His forever companion. Remember, once you have made the decision to accept Jesus as your personal Savior you are called to a life of pursuing righteousness. That prepares you for His return.

However, there are three things that can trip you along the way: Satan, the world, and your flesh. There are also three things that have already saved you from them. First, in the Father's grace, love and mercy he has provided the armor you need to battle them and we will discuss them in this chapter. Next, the Holy Spirit in you is your guide and companion through the jabs at your heart from your enemies. Last and very important, Jesus has already conquered all of your enemies. Yes, I said it; they are already defeated! That's the good news. The bad news is that we do not act like it. We act like the battle is too tough for us. We whine, complain and give up so many times. We do not use the armor that God has provided for us to pursue that life of righteousness. Let me explain myself …

Imagine yourself one of these two ways. One, you are a bride walking down the aisle of righteousness. You are on the arm of the Father. Jesus is at the end of the aisle waiting for you. The Holy Spirit is the best man. You are perfectly dressed in white fine linen. You approach the throne and take Jesus' hand. He says, "You are a most beautiful bride." Then he notices you smiling and questions what is making you so happy. You lift up the hem of your wedding garment and show Him your shoes. They are your dancing shoes, the same shoes you used all of your life dancing with Him. These shoes are worn, torn, and very precious to you. Jesus smiles back (remember you live for those smiles!) and you start to dance with Him.

Second, you are a Bride walking down the aisle. You are holding something in your hand and cannot hold onto the arm of the Father. You can barely see Jesus because your veil is crooked. The Holy Spirit is trying to help you down the aisle because your dress is in the way. It doesn't seem to fit. You enter the throne room and take a seat on the nearest step. Jesus looks at you and says, "Are you my bride?" You reply, "Yes, I am." He then asks, "What are you holding in your hands?" You say," Oh, these are my shoes. They are killing my feet."

Do you understand what I am trying to say? Your spiritual life today is preparing you for eternity with Jesus. What kind of bride do you plan to be? One who cherishes His commands and yearns to know Him better or one who the enemy has a hold on? You have to make that choice today and everyday.

Our gracious Father has provided us with many weapons to help us down the aisle of righteousness. We are given spiritual clothes and equipment to use in the fight. However, you have to use them for them to feel comfortable to you. Once you have seen the power of prayer you will continue to pray. When you claim a promise for yourself from His Word you are never again the same. When you use God's strength to battle the enemy you are confident in Him. You are then on your way to becoming a prepared bride for Jesus. God is then very proud of you. Let me give you another example....

Look at me Daddy!

My husband wears baseball caps a lot. His favorite cap has his company logo and name on it. He will put it on our three-year-old little boy's head and then smile as he sees his future business partner under that big cap. We love to see little Stevie's dimples the minute it goes on his head. You cannot see his eyes, just his big dimples. He feels like daddy under that hat and he knows that is special.

It touches my husband when little Stevie will grab the hat and run into the room with a big smile...Look at me daddy! I want to be just like you! My husband can find no better joy than that. That is how God feels when we dress like Him. We put on the belt of truth, the breastplate of righteousness, the shoes of peace, the sword of truth and the shield of faith and He feels so proud. Look at me, Daddy! I want to be just like you! Dressing like Daddy is an important part of every Christian's life.

Therefore put on the full armor of God, so that when the day of evil comes, you may be able to stand your ground, and after you have done everything, to stand. Stand firm then, with the belt of truth buckled around your waist, with the breastplate of righteousness in place, and with your feet fitted with the readiness that comes from the gospel of peace. In addition to all this, take up the shield of faith with which you can extinguish all the flaming arrows of the evil one. Take the helmet of salvation and the sword of the Spirit which is the word of God. (Ephesians 6: 13-17)

The Full Armor

God has given us this armor so that we can be prepared for battle from Satan and the spiritual world that is against us. *For our struggle is not against flesh and blood, but against the powers of this dark world and against the spiritual forces of evil in the heavenly realms.* (Ephesians 6:12) We need to put our full armor on everyday with *confidence*. Satan then looks at us and sees God. He cannot touch God with his evil. He sees Daddy's hat, shoes, belt and shirt and knows that he can do nothing. We may peek through the side of the shield and let Satan see us *scared* or we can *stand firm* as the Word says and *pray*. *And pray in the spirit on all occasions with all kinds of prayers and requests. With this in mind, be alert and always keep on praying for all the saints.* (Ephesians 6:18)

There are two things that Satan keeps himself busy with, deceiving and discouraging. Satan is your enemy. Satan is God's enemy. However, God has equipped every believer with weapons for these attacks. God has prepared us for spiritual battles in which we are dressed to win. You see God has already won this war because of the cross. We are only walking through a battleground that has been conquered! Satan doesn't want you to know that.

In Ephesians 6:18 above we see that he wants us to pray for each other. Satan is beaten down by believers praying the Word of God. All good soldiers fight for the same cause. Let's fight for the truth! We do not need to be rebuked. We need to be informed. So, let's take a quick look at each piece of armor and prepare for victory!

The belt of truth keeps us guarded from Satan's lies. Jesus, the Word of God, and the Holy Spirit are the truths that will support you in battles. When you are grounded in truth you are more prepared for spiritual battles. In Jesus you will find the way to that truth.

Jesus answered, I am the way and the truth and the life. No one comes to the Father except through me. (John 14: 6) Jesus says the truth shall set you free! *If you hold on to my teaching, you are really my disciples. Then you will know the truth and the truth shall set you free*. (John 8:32) Free from what? Free from the lies and bondage of Satan.

Knowing the Word of God is the truth that holds all of the pieces of armor in their places. *Sanctify them by the truth; your word is truth*. (John 17:17) The Word of God will be your support through all trials and hardships. This is how God teaches you His ways. When you follow the Master you will be used to His strategic planning. His game plan always comes from the truth, His Holy Word. The Holy Spirit will confirm the game plan to you. *And I will ask the Father and he will give you another Counselor to be with you forever - the Spirit of truth*. (John 14:16-17) V-I-C-T-O-R-Y is assured!

The breastplate of righteousness is something that we do not have on our own. This piece of armor is a precious gift from God. He has in His grace and mercy decided to consider us righteous because of what Jesus did for us on the cross. *God made him who had no sin to be sin for us, so that in him we might become the righteousness of God*. (2 Corinthians 5: 21) The breastplate was used in ancient battles to guard the vital organs. For Christians this is used to guard our hearts against the attacks of our enemies. *Above all else, guard your heart, for it is the wellspring of life*. (Proverbs 4:23) Our heart is important to God. Our heart is where he lives.

The gospel of peace (shoes) is important for soldiers to keep on marching. There can be many obstacles on the road to peace that can keep you from continuing your battle. Satan can trap you or trip your feet along the way. It is the peace that our Lord Jesus gives us that keep us going. *And the peace of God, which transcends all understanding, will guard your hearts and your minds in Christ.* (Philippians 4:7) Keep marching!

The shield of faith seems to be the most important part. You are to use it to shield yourself from Satan's flaming arrows or fiery darts! *In addition to all this, take up the shield of faith, with which you can extinguish all the flaming arrows of the evil one.* (Ephesians 6:16) These darts can be opposition, accusations, lies, deception, discouragement, or temptation! We are to have faith in Jesus not ourselves. We never want to go into battle in our own strength. We are to trust that what God has said in His Word is true. We are to live by faith. Faith that He has already conquered all for us. *For in the gospel a righteousness from God is revealed, a righteousness that is by faith from first to last, just as it is written: "The righteous will live by faith."* (Romans 1: 17)

The helmet of salvation is our headgear. We are to be guarded against the thoughts and lies that Satan can put in our minds. I get so worried when I see someone on a bike or motorcycle without his helmet on. He is not protected from the danger of head injuries. Satan is the master of mind games. We are to wear our protection of salvation to resist his dark whispers. Look only to Jesus. *Salvation is found in no one else, for there is no other name under heaven given to men by which to be saved.* (Acts 4:12) Keep your mind and thoughts only on the things that God would want you to. *Finally, brothers, whatever is true, whatever is right, whatever is admirable-if anything is excellent or praiseworthy-think about such things.* (Philippians 4:8) Next, take a look at 2 Corinthians 10:5, *We demolish arguments and* *every pretension that sets itself up against the knowledge of Christ. Every thought must be obedient to Christ.* Every thought must be obedient to Christ, think about that!

The sword of the Spirit is the Word of God. Of all the armor, this is the only one that we use offensively. The Word of God is our weapon. *For the word of God is living and active. Sharper than any double-edged sword.* (Hebrews 4:12) The Word of God is an obstacle to Satan. God's Word exposes Satan as a liar. The mention of God's promises is threatening to him. Talking like Daddy keeps Satan powerless. You can get out of Satan's snare by praying and acting on God's word. When you return God's Word to Him in prayer He will perform it. When you speak the truth Satan will flee. *Resist the devil and he will flee from you.* (James 4:7)

The Holy Scripture is the most powerful weapon given to the Church. It happens to also be the most under used. This battle is spiritual and needs to be fought in God's strength. *If you remain in me and my words remain in you, ask whatever you wish and, and it will be given to you.* (John 15:7) Don't you think it's important to know the words of Daddy! His words spoke creation into being, that's pretty powerful!

Be Alert and Keep Praying!

There are few more things that I want you to think about. One, is there any armor for our back? The answer is no. If we do not stand firm and resist Satan then we are vulnerable to his attack. If you turn your back and run, you are wide open for one of his fiery arrows. Let me tell you something: those attacks are real and powerful. I am sure that you agree with me on that!

Secondly, what are we to do once we are equipped in our full armor? Remember this verse: *And pray in the spirit on all occasions with all kinds of prayers and requests. With this in mind, be alert and always keep praying for all the saints.* (Ephesians 6:18) Be alert and keep praying! Prayer is another offensive weapon that is very powerful when used. Oswald Chambers said it best, "Prayer does not equip you for greater works, it is the greater work." Prayer is the weapon Satan fears most. So, obviously it is his most targeted war zone. Prayer-less lives are powerless lives. Praying the Word of God is the most effective weapon you will ever know. Try it. You'll like it!

Lastly, does scripture ever tell us to take off our armor? No, we are to keep it on always! We aren't to take it off before bedtime or even a bath! We are to put it on and keep it secure and in place daily!

Staying alert and knowing your position in Christ is very important. The spiritual battle is for God and His strength. The battle is the Lord's. *All those gathered here will know that it is not by sword or spear that the Lord saves; for the battle is the Lord's, and he will give all into your hands.* (1 Samuel 17:47) His strength is your strength. You are a child of God and nothing can touch you that hasn't been through the throne room for approval first.

You have to be confident in understanding your identity! God has done tremendous things for you. You are a servant of God and accepted in His presence through the blood of Jesus. You are now sitting in a position of royalty. Resist Satan! When you are walking in God's love you are far, far, far from bondage! FAR!

Winning the War

If nothing can touch us that hasn't sifted through God's hands why would He allow these attacks? What do we gain from these fiery darts? Hey, isn't He on our side? Why would He allow shots at His own soldiers? Have those thoughts ever crossed your mind? Let me answer those questions for you. God has already won the war! He is allowing battles for our own personal growth. Our falls build stronger character. He uses our battle scars to equip other soldiers. Practice makes a perfect bride! We then encourage others to walk where He has already conquered. They do the same for others. Soldiers are then more plentiful and strong.

That is major strategic planning on God's part! He is reminding us that He has won the war by allowing battles. God has brought priceless things out of my personal battle with our three hindrances: Satan, the world, and flesh. I could never have received those treasures in my own flesh. They have to be through the power of God.

The way to win the war is remembering that the battle is God's not yours! He will reward you for letting Him do all the work. You just need to show up for the battle dressed and ready to go!

The priceless jewels such as joy, strength, peace, love, kindness, nobility, gentleness, compassion, patience are characteristics He is looking for in a bride. They are God's medals of honor to give His soldiers for persevering. Battles build Christ-like character in the Bride and win souls for the Bridegroom. Press on! Dance on!

Chapter Four Study Questions

Before you begin for the wisdom and discernment needed to study His Holy Word!

Lets study a little bit here about our enemy.

Read Ephesians 2:1-2 and fill in the blanks:

As for you, you were dead in your trespasses and sins, in which you used to live when you walked the ways of this world and the prince of the kingdom of air, the spirit who is now at work in those who are disobedient.

What control does Satan have in those who are disobedient? He works in them.

Read 2 Corinthians 11:14-15 for some very important information!

What does Satan masquerade as?

an angel of light

What does this mean?

He acts like a minister.

Read 2 Corinthians 4:4 and fill in the blanks:

The god of this age has blended the minds of non-believers, so that they cannot see the light of the gospel of the glory of Christ, who is the image of God.

What does Satan do to unbelievers?

He blinds them to the truth.

How is Satan described in 1Thessalonains 3:5?

a tempter

Write out and read aloud Ephesians 1:13-14.

We have been sealed w/ the Holy Spirit

Whom has God sealed you with?

Holy Spirit

When you are sealed with Christ it places you in a position of power. You can resist Satan!!

Read Ephesians 1:18-20 and fill in the blanks:

I pray also that the eyes of your understanding may be enlightened in order that you may know the hope to which he called you, the riches of his glorious inheritance in the saints, and his exceeding great power for us who believe. That power is like the working of his mighty strength, which he exerted in Christ when he raised him from the dead and seated him at his right hand in the heavenly realms.

Where is Jesus now?

heaven

Let's read further write out Ephesians 1:21-23!

Let's look again at verse 22, *And God placed all things under his feet and appointed him to be head over everything for the church.* Jesus has power over all rule and authority. That includes Satan and his demons. Deception and discouragement are Satan's only weapons. If Jesus lives in your heart you have authority over them as well. All you have to do is say Jesus' name and His power flows!

Read John 16:24. Oh, the joy of belonging to Jesus.

What does Ephesians 2:19-20 say about Jesus?

Chief cornerstone

Satan has limits! Read Luke 22:31.

Satan asked to sift Peter as wheat. However, did you notice what Jesus did for Him? He prayed for Him. Jesus being the cornerstone to your faith, sitting at the right hand of the Father with all power and authority intercedes for you daily. You can conquer all.

John 17 is Jesus' prayer is for you. Write out John 17:15.

What does Daniel 4:35 say about God's sovereignty?

No one can restrain His Hand.

Read 1 Peter 5:6-9 and fill in the blanks:
(6-7)
humble yourselves, therefore, under God's mighty hand, that he may lift you up in due time. Cast all your anxiety on him because he cares for you.

Why cast all your anxiety on God? He cares for me.

(8) Be sober-vigilant and ______. Your adversary the devil prowls around like a roaring lion looking for someone to devour.

What is your responsibility in this verse? sober vigilant

What command does verse 9 give us? Resist the devil

Read 1 Corinthians 10:13b and fill in the blanks:

And God is faithful; he will not let you be tempted beyond what you can handle. But when you are tempted, he will also make a way of escape so that you can bear it under it.

God will provide a way out so that you can stand up under it!

Let's look further at our Full Armor: Read Ephesians 6:10-20.

Who is our struggle with?

the devil

This scripture tells us to put on our full armor of God, so that when (not if) the day of evil comes, you may be able to stand your ground, and after you have done everything, to stand. We cannot put on one or two pieces of armor. This scripture commands us to do them all, then stand!

Let's review the armor again:

The belt of truth is what sets the captives free! Let's confirm that by writing out John 8:36!

we will be free

How do you receive the breastplate of righteousness? (2 Corinthians 5:21)

through Jesus

How are the shoes of peace described in Romans 10:15?

beautiful feet

What does the shield of faith do? (Ephesians 6:16)

quench the fiery darts of the wicked one

The helmet of salvation is our headgear. Whose mind do you have? (1 Corinthians 2:16)

the Lord

What three things are we commanded to do in 1 Peter 1:13?

1. gird up the loins of your mind
2. be sober
3. rest your hope

How do we do these things?

by living for Christ

Read 2 Timothy 1:7 and fill in the blanks:

For God did not give us a spirit of __fear__, but a spirit of __power__, of __love__ and of __a sound mind__.

We can exchange the spirit of timidity with the spirit of power and the spirit of love and the spirit of self-discipline! Thank you, Jesus!

What is the sword of the Spirit? (Ephesians 6:17)

the word of God

Write out Colossians 3:16.

Close in prayer.

Chapter Five

Daddy's Girl

"How great is the love the Father has lavished on us, that we should be called children of God! And that is what we are!"
(1 John 3:1)

There is a story about a beautiful dancer with the New York City Ballet. She was described by some critics as easily distracted by a lack of confidence. Then Mikhail Baryshnikov chose her as his partner and her reviews changed to, "exhilarating," "sensational," and even "breathtaking!" He brought out the best in her. She was never as outstanding with any other dancer. Only him.[1]

The same goes for you! The Master has chosen you! Do you mind if I say that again? You have been chosen by The Master! He has chosen you to be His dance partner for life. Your dance will then be exhilarating, sensational, even breathtaking! You will never be outstanding with another partner. Submit to His lead! Let His moves be your moves! Let His steps be your steps!

Sometimes your dance will be slow, with Him holding you close. The song might be melancholy and He will just want to hold you! Other times, He will let you dance at arms' length while he is teaching you His ways. Other times He will let you go from His arms. It is then that

---

[1]Thank you to Dr. Joe Brown's sermon!

your steps have to be identical to His. You will be exactly mirroring His steps because you will know Him so well. You will be mirroring His steps because you will want to please Him. You will be mirroring His steps because you and He are one. A perfect dance with the master!

Characteristics of Daddy's Girl

Dancing with God keeps you close to the Father of your dreams. God represents fatherhood, not man. You will never know true fatherhood until you know God intimately as Father. It is earthly fathers who are to mirror God, not vice-versa. God, your Creator, your Father, planned before the beginning of time to nurture you, protect you, provide for you, comfort you, encourage you, train you and love you. You are the apple of His eye. *Keep me as the apple of your eye; hide me in the shadow of your wings.* (Psalm 17:8)

Feeling love from the hand of God is what carries us through the aches in our tender hearts. The Father's tender kindness will mend any insecurity or doubt that the world may throw your way. Being a child of God guarantees you every promise written in the Bible. You are to possess your inheritance as a child of the King! You are a daughter of royalty. You are a royal princess.

Let's take a look at some of the personal characteristics of being Daddy's girl.

Knows her Father's voice

God speaks to His children. He talks to all of us in different ways. He has made us all unique and our relationship with Him is to be very personal. When God speaks you know it is from Him. You never want to miss a word from the lips of Daddy! His words are music to your ears.

He will speak to you through his Word, through others, praise songs, prayer, children, friends, spouses or maybe devotional books. He has even spoken to me through a Hollywood movie. He speaks to you in ways that only you would respond to. You see, it is your obedient response to His voice that distinguishes you as Daddy's little girl! Are you listening for His voice? Are you obedient to His word? If your answer to these questions is yes, then you have one proud Daddy! *My sheep listen to my voice; I know them, and they follow me*. (John10:27)

Knows that Father Knows Best

There are many times when we have to make decisions in life, such as whether or not to turn right or left. Choices are a big part of our lives. Do you stay home with your children? Do you change careers? Do you begin a new friendship? Do you marry the person you are dating? What do you do with your money? What do you do with your time? Who are you to confide in? What church do you serve at? How do you handle divorce? How do you handle single parenting? How do you handle a certain confrontation?

You may think that you are standing at the crossroads left wondering what to do. Let me assure you that the Father has a perfect plan for your life. He just requires that you seek Him. God wants you to know His will more than you do! Seek Him in all things.

Sometimes you will be asked by God to take a leap of faith as part of His plan. Using doubt, Satan will try to discourage you in your decision. Once you are confident that you have heard from God move forward. Take His lead. Take your dance lessons from the Father. He knows best! *Teach me to do your will, for you are my God; may your good Spirit lead me on level ground*. (Psalm 143:10)

Knows She Belongs to the Father

Do you know that you belong to the only person who can love you perfectly? The God who parted the Red Sea and placed it back can mend your broken heart. He works miraculously in all hopeless situations. Look forward to your miracle. It is on its way.

Belonging to God provides confidence for the saints. My daughter was scared of the possibility a hurricane was coming into our city. The only assurance I could positively give her was that we belong to God and He would take care of us. She slept like a baby that night. How will you sleep tonight? "*But you are a chosen people, a royal priesthood, a holy nation, a people belonging to God, that you may declare the praises of him who called you out of darkness into his wonderful light.*" (1 Peter 2:9)

Knows She Can Run to the Father When She Falls

When children fall and skin their knees they often react to their distress by running to their parents' arms. The same should happen to us when unexpected pain invades our lives. We should run to our Father with all of our bloody noses, black eyes, and skinned knees from the enemy.

I have found myself so hurt before that I couldn't move. I would just lie there and cry. That is when Daddy ran to me. Likewise, He wants to rescue you from all pain. Remember that Jesus died on the cross for your pain. God may heal you completely within a second of asking Him. Or, He may choose to work out His eternal purpose for you by allowing your pain to stay. We just have to have the faith that Daddy is working night and day on our behalf. He is a sovereign God, who is the lover of your soul, and will carry you through all your painful falls is your security. He has all the band-aids you need. *You are my hiding place; you will protect me from trouble and surround me with songs of deliverance.* (Psalm 32:7)

Knows Her Father is Everything to Her

There will come a time in our lives when something will try to take God's place. It may be your job, your husband, your friends, your hobbies, or even your children. All those things are the good gifts straight from Him. However, they are given to us to take pleasure in, not to worship. (Matthew 6:24)

You may not even know that something is taking God's place. I can promise you that as a child of God He will reveal it to you. You cannot dethrone God. He has to be everything to you! You will eventually find out that whatever you are holding onto closer than God will never fill the spot reserved for Him. You will be thankful for this revelation. No one can ever love you the way that Daddy can. *How awesome is the LORD Most High, the great King over all the earth!* (Psalm 47:2)

Knows to Follow Her Dreams

Do you have a God-size dream in your heart? Did you know that your Father wants your dreams to come true? When you love someone deeply you would do anything to provide for his or her dreams. Through Jesus, God has provided everything you need for your dreams to come true.

A God-size dream is what is said between your heart and God's. He can speak right to your heart and you can know that dream is from Him. The secret to grabbing hold of your dream is actually to release it. I had a vision of what a perfect plan would be for my ministry. It wasn't

God's. I had to let go of that dream. That is when He replaced it with His. He replaced it with a God-size dream, not a Sheila-size dream.

Would you ever want to live out a dream that wasn't from Him? No, because His dream is always 1000 times better than yours. You cannot dream God-size dreams without God. Do you have a dream? Keep dreaming. His dreams always come true. *In his heart a man plans his course, but the LORD determines steps.* (Proverbs 16:9)

Knows Her Father-Daughter Talks Nourish and Flourish Her

Prayer used to be something I did only in emergency situations. I thank Daddy that He has burdened me to pray all day long. We are to live a life of "praying without ceasing." There are times when He wakes me up in the middle of the night with someone on my mind. I will lie there and pray for that person. Other times I am asked to get out of bed and get on my knees to pray. (Obedience over a warm bed and husband is sacrifice!)

Prayer is not always petitioning God, but prayer *is* constantly talking to Him. Praying to God is like e-mail, a letter, card or a long phone call to a friend. It is talking to Him as the most important person in your life. You tell Him everything. He is your best friend. You are to live as if He was with you every second, because He is! Some of my prayers have been one-word prayers. (Usually, HELP!) By doing that it means you are including Him in your life.

You can pray by saying nothing at all. God knows your hurt even when you can't express it. I have a room in my house that I call the Holy of Holies. Whenever I am overwhelmed, I run to that room and pray face down. Normally when I am in that room to pray I am crying too hard to speak. I lie there in Jesus' arms while he prays to the

Father for me. Prayer is your way of putting faith in Him and Him alone. A Daddy's girl knows what pleases her Father. Our faith-filled prayers please Him. He loves when we come to Him for wisdom, encouragement, cleansing or even just to sit in His presence.

The other day Brittany came to me to tell me that a little girl in her class hurt her feelings. All she wanted was a "mom hug." It was a very special time. I look forward to many more bonding times. But I depend on her coming to me for them. I am sure you can parallel that to your Father-Daughter talks with God. Go to Him for a great big "Dad hug". He looks forward to them. He will nourish your soul and flourish your heart. *Be joyful always; pray continually; give thanks in all circumstances, for this is God's will for you in Christ Jesus.* (1 Thessalonians 5:16-18)

Knows She Looks Just Like Her Father

Can people see your heavenly Father in you? The highest compliment that anyone can ever give you on earth is that you mirror Jesus. "Are you the daughter of the Great Physician, the King of Kings, the Prince of Peace, the Great I Am, the Alpha, the Omega?" Your reply, "Yes, I am!" They respond back, "You are the spitting image of Him! You have His peace, joy, love, wisdom, patience, kindness, and strength all over your face! I could tell you belonged to Him right away!" Does that put a smile on your face? Daddy sure has one! *This is to my Father's glory, that you bear much fruit, showing yourselves to be disciples.* (John 15:8)

Knows That the Father Thinks She's Beautiful.

Our heavenly Father adores you. His adoring eyes watch your every move. You are at the center of His attention. He smiles when you laugh. His tears fall when yours do. You have a Father who thinks you are absolutely beautiful. In fact, scripture says that He is enthralled with your beauty! There will be nothing more special than you and the Father dancing in eternity while He whispers in your ear, "You are so beautiful to me my child!" For now, just know that He is on the throne ruling the world and taking pleasure in your beauty! *The king is enthralled by your beauty; honor him for he is your lord.* (Psalm 45:11)

Are you a Daddy's girl?

Chapter Five Study Questions

Before you begin pray for the wisdom and discernment needed to study His Holy Word.

Write out 1 John 3:1 What manner of love the Father has bestowed on us that we should be called children of God.

Read John 10:29 and fill in the blanks:
My Father, who has __given__ them to __me__, is __greater__ than __all__ no one can __snatch__ them out of my Father's __hand__.

Read John 17:23. God loves you the same as He loves Jesus!

Read Psalm 145:8-21 and write out some of the attributes of God.

Did you find out that your Father is gracious, compassionate, slow to anger, rich in love, good to all, faithful, loving, and righteous? Do you mirror the Father?

Fill in the blanks to the following verses from Psalm 145:

(14) The LORD __upholds__ all those who __fall__ and __raises__ __up__ all who are __bowed__ down.

(18) The LORD is __near__ to all who __call__ on Him, to all who call on Him in __truth__.

(19) He fulfills the desires of those who fear Him; He hears their cry and saves them.

Call on God in truth and He will lift your sad face up and grant you your dream, the desires of your heart! Praise Daddy!

Read 1 Kings 19:11-13. How was God's voice described here? Is that how you hear His voice?

Still small voice

What does Isaiah 30:21 say about God speaking to us? Are you listening for His voice? He speaks behind us.

Read Colossians 3:1-17 for some more of the characteristics of a Daddy girl.

What should our minds be set on?

things above

From verse 5 list some things that need to be put to death:

1. fornication
2. uncleanness
3. passion
4. evil desire
5. covetousness

Which is idolatry.

Why? (verse 6) Because the wrath of God will come . . .

What should you rid yourself of? (verse 8)

1. anger
2. wrath
3. malice
4. blasphemy
5. filthy lang.

Fill in the blanks from verse 9:

Do not lie to each other, since you have taken off your old self with its practices and have put on your new self, which is being renewed in knowledge in the image of its Creator.

What should we, as God's chosen people clothe ourselves with? (verse 12)

1. tender mercies
2. kindness
3. humility
4. meekness
5. longsuffering

Do not forget to follow the commandment in verse 13! Forgive as the Lord forgave you!

Write out verse 14.

What should rule in your heart? (verse 15)

peace of God

What does that verse say you were called to?

one body

What is to dwell in us richly? (verse16)

word of Christ

Whose name do we do all of these things in? (verse17)

Lord Jesus

Let's list some other characteristics of a Daddy's girl. (Galatians 5:22-23) love, joy, peace, long-suff. kindness goodness, faithfulness, gentleness, self-control

Write out Matthew 7:20.

by their fruits you know them.

Fruit is the evidence that you are a child of the King!

Write out John 10:37. The works of the Father are by Jesus Christ.

Read Philippians 1:9-10. Where does the fruit of righteousness come from?

Jesus Christ

Read Ephesians 1:4-5 and fill in the blanks:

For He chose us ___ him before the ____________ of the _______ to be holy and blameless in his sight. In love He _________ us to be _________ as his sons through ______ ______, in accordance with his ________ and ______- to the praise of his glorious ______, which he has freely given us in the one he loves.

That's a powerful verse. It tells of our family history. Let's list them.

1. He chose us in Him before the creation of the world.
2. He chose us to be holy and blameless in His sight.
3. In love He predestined us to be adopted as His sons.
4. We are part of God's family because of Jesus Christ. We are part of God's family because it is His will. We are part of God's family because it is His pleasure.
5. It is by His grace through Jesus Christ we are adopted into His family.

Last, I want you to look at a sweet scripture verse in Hosea. It is a verse that portrays our loving Father.

It was I who taught Ephraim to walk, taking them by the arms. (Hosea 11:3)

Is Daddy teaching you to walk? Are you allowing Him to walk in His ways? You must make your Daddy proud!

Close in prayer.

Chapter Six

Heavenly Education

May God himself, the God of peace,
sanctify you through and through.
May your whole spirit, soul and body be kept blameless
at the coming of our Lord Jesus Christ.
The one who calls you is faithful and he will do it.
(1Thessalonians 5:23-24)

I have danced to the sad song of fear and anxiety for a big part of my life. These are feelings that we all look to get away from. We are looking to the right, looking to the left and to the end of the road for the next turn called escape. We find ourselves frantically trying to take control of our "disaster of a life." We never ever look behind because what we are hiding from others is there. We are forever manipulating and designing a cure for our pain.

If I had been grounded in the truth and dressed with Christ's righteousness I could have been more prepared for my opposition that was sure to come my way. There are many things that I have learned through my battles that I am happy to share with you, so that your road will be shorter and wiser. Don't forget it is the victories of God's soldiers that He uses to encourage others. Let me tell you how my dance to the song of freedom started. Whatever you are going through will fit right into this dance lesson. I have found the answer to all the pains in life. So, listen up!

Lesson #1: Your Cure is Always Temporary.

But when the kindness and love of God our Savior appeared, he saved us, not because of righteous things we had done, but because of his mercy. (Titus 3:4-5)

I was so affected by my father's death that I was scared of life. I decided that I had to avoid going through that pain again at all costs. It seemed the smartest thing for me to do. I believed that if I had planned better for the first time disaster hit my family that my father might not have committed suicide. The pressure of an uncontrolled life was the end for me. This is when I became anorexic and then bulimic. My eating disorders started within a year of my father's death and lasted until the third year of my marriage.

Now there were two things that I was hiding from others: pain and an eating disorder. These deceptions were now my life. I was obsessed with the day-to-day control of it. I was achieving control and deceiving others through manipulation. I felt as though I was finally accomplishing something. If awards were given out for this kind of deception I would have an Oscar. Remember, there are two things that the prince of this world (Satan) tries to do to us, deceive us and discourage us. I was totally deceived. I had no idea that he was keeping me from truth. That's when Jesus showed up!

Lesson #2: When You Wrestle with Satan, Pin Him!

I am the light of the world. Whoever follows me will never walk in darkness, but have the light of life. (John 8:12)

I had never noticed Jesus before that day. The veil had been lifted from my face. Jesus stepped in front of Satan, picked me up out of darkness, and brought me into His light. He gave me enough light to see myself in chains and bondage. I was shocked! I wanted out of these chains! Satan had lied to me! I knew that in my heart and wanted desperately to be released from him. I realized that I had given him permission to deceive me. I was in total darkness. Now the light of truth was drawing me to Jesus and I wanted it as I had never wanted anything else in my life. I felt that I had to be out of the chains in order to reach for it. How was I to do that? I was ashamed of what I had done. I realized that I was sinning against God. I was serving another, obsessed with something, and abusing His temple. My husband and I had been trying for a long time to have a baby and now I knew why I wasn't pregnant. I was killing myself.

I tried so hard to get the chains off. I wrestled with them morning, noon, and night. The more I tried the heavier they got. I pulled out my best chain saw. There were more chains added. I was determined to beat this thing. I kept reporting back to God that I was trying my hardest to get to Him and I would be there as quick as I could. Finally, there were so many chains around me that I couldn't move. The exhaustion of my wrestling had me crying. *In my distress I called to the LORD; I cried to my God for help. From his temple he heard my voice; my cry came before him, into his ears.* (Psalm 18:6)

" Jesus," I said, " I have tried everything that I know how to get these chains off. What do I do? I do not want to be this way forever. Help me! I am miserable. I want to feel freedom!" Jesus then healed me completely. I've never known such tenderness with strength. My chains were gone and I was free. Forever! I was taken from Satan by the power of God because I cried out to Him. *He rescued me from my powerful enemy, from my foes who were too strong for me.* (Psalm 18:17)

I could tell this pleased Jesus. It surprised me that I was the one receiving the healing, yet Jesus made me feel that he was the one receiving the gift. That is perfect love.

Lesson #3: God Allows Pain to Drive You to Jesus!

It was good for me to be afflicted so that I might learn your decrees. (Psalm 119:71)

That's when I found the answer to pain. Give it to Him. All I had to do was give it to Him. I'll say it one more time, GIVE IT TO HIM! You see, we cannot do things in our own strength. Those solutions will only be temporary. If you do happen to conquer your battle, then your problem will just be transferred to another war zone. His love is what conquers. *There is no fear in love. But perfect love drives out fear, because fear has to do with punishment. The one who fears is not made perfect in love.* (1 John 4:18) Perfect love casts out fear. Perfect love is found only in Him.

When you belong to Him all that comes your way has been sifted through hands that love you perfectly. Even if those times are tough they were permitted for your ultimate good. It has taken a lot of tough times for me to understand that. Remember that battles are allowed for the making of character, which should ultimately be more and more Christ-like. *And we, who with unveiled faces all reflect the Lord's glory, are being transformed into his likeness with ever-increasing glory, which comes from the Lord, who is the Spirit.* (2 Corinthians 3:18)

Satan lies to us about achieving happiness in life. Happiness from him is money, children, husbands, looks, cars, homes, clothes, religion, success, prestige, recognition, fame, people-pleasing, popularity, or addictions. I was enjoying that satisfaction only because I was deceived. Therefore, I was being kept from the ultimate satisfaction of knowing my Savior. Satan's goal is to keep you away from knowing Jesus. You may be deceived with drugs, alcohol, sex, food or any of the things listed above. If so, you are in bondage to Satan and his lies. You can be in bondage in a big way like alcoholism or in a small way like perfectionism. Either way it's bondage and you are being kept from the greatest satisfaction of all: Knowing Jesus. You cannot live a full life without Jesus Christ. Worldly things will not make you happy. There is an emptiness in your soul that only the Holy Spirit can fit into perfectly.

You can try to fit other things in there but they won't fit. The size needed to fill that emptiness is only known by God. That piece of the puzzle to your heart is His. He has the exclusive rights to it. He has the patent to it because he made you. *Is he not your Father, your Creator, who made you and formed you?* (Deuteronomy 32: 6) He chose you to be his. *Yet to all who have who have received him, to those who believed in his name, he gave the right to become children of God – children born not of natural descent, nor of human decision or a husband's will, but born of God.* (John 1:12-13) He is drawing you to Him. *No one can come to me unless the Father who sent me draws him, and I will raise him up at the last day.* (John 6:44) The ultimate decision is yours. *Submit yourselves, then, to God. Resist the devil and he will flee from you. Come near to God and he will come near to you.* (James 4: 7-8) Will you submit? Will you let him have complete control of your life? Will you resist Satan and draw near to God? If so, you will find perfect peace.

Lesson #4: Satan is Out to Destroy You. But, Jesus has Already Delivered You From Darkness.

He brought them out of darkness and the deepest gloom and broke away their chains. Let them give thanks to the LORD for his unfailing love and his wonderful deeds for men.
(Psalm 107:14-15)

Satan must be a pretty deceitful creature to have taken one third of the angels with him. We read in the Bible that we do not struggle with flesh and blood, but against the spiritual world. We are reading about the fighting going on between the angels who work for God and the demons that work for Satan. There is a struggle going on in the spiritual world around us that we cannot see.

Satan is attacking the very heart of God when he attacks the church. However, it is the free will of man that keeps this battle going. If it were not for our free will God would end this battle with a blink of his eye or the snap of his finger. He has that power! He has given us the position in Christ that we need to conquer evil. *I have given you authority to trample on snakes and scorpions and to overcome all the power of the enemy: nothing will harm you.* (Luke 10:19) The power is in Jesus' name alone. Are you using Jesus' name?

If Satan is deceiving you with the happiness of this world or binding you to his chains please run to Jesus! He is the only one who can set you free. I was not walking with Him when I was bound to Satan's lies. Jesus as my Savior was very real to me. However, the freedom did not come until he became Lord of my life.

We all seem to do the "Christian Hokey-Pokey." We never give Him our whole self. That is the key to a victorious Christian life, submitting all to Jesus. Don't dance the Hokey–Pokey with Him. Dance your whole life to His music. Dance to His grace, mercy and love. Give Him control of your song. He will be your faithful friend and your deliver.

Lesson #5: God's Cures are Permanent!

Praise the LORD, O my soul; all my inmost being, praise his holy name. Praise the LORD, O my soul, and forget not all his benefits-who forgives all your sins and heals all your diseases, who redeems your life from the pit and crowns you with love and compassion. (Psalm 103:1-4)

I have never had to battle eating disorders ever since the day Jesus freed me. People often ask me, "How do you handle fasting? How do you handle cooking for your family or eating out with friends?" I really have a hard time answering because I can't explain His power to them. I realize that it's hard to believe unless you have received it yourself. All I know is that they can receive the same healing power as I did for anything they need. Jesus is the Great Physician. When He heals He heals completely.

I was released from that bondage. There is no continued struggle. There are no worries of falling back into that bondage. Some people say, "Once an alcoholic always an alcoholic." Well, not true if freed by Jesus Christ! If the Son has set you free, you are free indeed!

It's amazing to feel that freedom. It's more than I ever imagined it could be. When some one asks me "How did you overcome your eating disorder?" I tell them, "By the blood of Jesus! That freedom was purchased for me at the cross." The same has been done for you! If Jesus never did another thing for you He has already done enough because of the cross! You can be free!

Living in the light gives you such peace. It gives you the victory that the cross represents. *And having disarmed the powers and authorities, he made a public spectacle of them, triumphing over them by the cross.* (Colossians 2:15) Freedom is a precious word to my heart. I cannot believe that more people aren't claiming their victories. Are you? *The weapons we fight with are not the weapons of this world. On the contrary, they have divine power to demolish strongholds.* (2 Corinthians 10:4)

My healing didn't stop at the eating disorder. One week after my healing, we found out that I was four weeks pregnant with our first child. *Stretch out your hand to heal and perform miraculous signs and wonders through the name of your holy servant Jesus.* (Acts 4:30) She's eight years old now. The blessings from knowing and trusting in God are true miracles. My sins were forgiven even before my life began. My blessings were on their way before my healing was even asked for.

I love sharing with others the wonderful story of His love. It is a sweet story to Him. I believe that every time we share our testimony He holds His holy hand up for creation to be silent so that He can hear the sweetest love story ever told. We are all Daddy's favorite child. He does not love any of us more than He does another. However, He is more intimate with some. That, my friend, is your choice. Are you intimate with Him? I was a lemon until the living water was poured on me. Then Daddy added His sugar and now I am His lemonade. Would you like to be more intimate with Him? He hopes so!

Lesson #6: You are a Loved Child of God!

"*For you created my inmost being; you knit me together in my mother's womb. I praise you because I am fearfully and wonderfully made; your works are wonderful. I know that full well.*" (Psalm139:13-14)

We seem to be more aware of who Satan tells us we are than of what God has told us. The question today is who are you going to believe? Satan or *God*? (I gave you a big hint there!) If we are to believe God's word is true then probably our whole way of thinking has to change. People have a hard time believing that they are important to God. We believe that we are not truly loved. Like my old self, we believe that God is far off and that He is busy with others. We are deceived into believing that we are a nobody. How can we be a nobody when God has made us for Himself?

Satan lies to us and tells us that what we have done in the past or what we are doing now is keeping God from loving us. He puts us on an imaginary probation period. We believe that we have to do something to clean up our act before we can come before the throne of God. Lie! Lie! Lie! The only thing we need to approach the throne is the blood of Jesus. Nothing can then separate us from the love of God. *For I am convinced that neither death nor life, neither angel nor demons, neither the present nor the future, nor any powers, neither height nor depth, nor anything in all creation, will be able to separate us from the love of God that is in Christ Jesus our Lord.* (Romans 8:38)

Jesus paid a debt *you owed.* That is the key part to our faith. Jesus took our place in death to sin. *Just as man is destined to die once, and after that face judgment, so Christ was sacrificed once to take away the sins of many people; and he will appear a second time, not to bear sin, but to bring salvation to those who are waiting on him.* (Hebrews 9:28) He was the perfect heavenly sacrifice. *Without the shedding of blood there is no forgiveness.* (Hebrews 9:22)

My husband and I have learned through the years to always buy the more quality product over the less expensive. We agree with the motto, "You get what you pay for!" Jesus Christ must have thought a whole lot of you to have paid the very dear price of His own life for you. He risked His very throne by coming to earth to purchase you! Satan is furious at that. Of course he wants you to never realize that truth. It is Satan's plan to deceive God's children. Don't let him! God has gone to great lengths to prove His love. Think about that the next time you hear from Satan.

Lesson #7: You Are Either Slave to Sin or Slave to Righteousness and It's Your Choice Which One.

You have been set free from sin and have become slaves to righteousness. (Romans 6:18)

This last lesson is a major one. We will devote much of the rest of the book on it. Isaiah 64:6 tells us, *All of us have become like one who is unclean, and all our righteous acts are like filthy rags*. Romans 3:10 tells us that no one is righteous not one! Once we are covered by the blood of Jesus we are righteous in the eyes of God. We are then slaves to righteousness. (Romans 6:18) *God made him who had no sin to be sin for us, so that in him we might become the righteousness of God*. (2 Corinthians 5:21)

We are most definitely slaves to righteousness. I don't have to tell you the gut-wrenching feeling you have in your stomach when you sin. The Spirit will convict you of your sin every single time! Let's define sin a little clearer here. Sin is anything that does not glorify God.

We are to live to glorify God and any thing that doesn't will be revealed to us by what I call a "stomach bug!" The bug will not go away until you do something about it. (Repent and turn back towards the righteousness of God!) A dance lesson for the kingdom is what I call it. Being a slave to righteousness is what prepares you as Jesus' bride.

Now, let's review our dance steps.

1. Your cure to the pains in life is always temporary.
2. When you wrestle with Satan, pin him!
3. God allows pain to drive you to Jesus!
4. Satan is out to destroy you. But, Jesus has already delivered you from darkness.
5. God's cures to the pains in life are always permanent!
6. You are a loved child of God!
7. You are either slave to sin or slave to righteousness and it's your choice which one.

Now, tell Fred Astaire to move over. You have mastered these dance steps!

Chapter Six Study Questions

Pray before you begin for the wisdom and discernment needed to study His Holy Word!

Read Psalm 139. Fill in the blanks to the following verses. (1-4)
O LORD, you have __________ me and you __________ me. You know when I ________ and when I ________; you perceive my ____________ from afar. You__________ my going out and my lying down; you are familiar with ______ my ______. Before a ______ is on my ________ you know it __________, O LORD.

Read Psalm 139: 13 and 14 again and fill in the blanks: (13-14)
For you __________ my inmost being; you ______ me __________ in my mother's ________. I ________ you because I am __________ and __________ made: your works are __________, I know that full well.

Do you believe God's works are wonderful? You are His work! You must be wonderful!

Write out verse Psalm 139:17.

How often does God think of you?

Read Psalm 139:7 again:
Where can I go from your Spirit? Where can I flee from your presence?

There is no hiding from God! The key to victory in Christ is acknowledging your weaknesses and sin before Him. Once you have done that He is obligated to free you and redeem you.

Write out Hebrews 10:23 for confirmation on that!

He is faithful!

Write out and read aloud Jeremiah 32:17. Why should we give all of our concerns to God? Nothing is too hard for God.

Write out and read aloud Mark 9:23. What is the prerequisite to the impossible?

all things are possible w/ God

Write out and read aloud Matthew 14:28-29

Peter walked on water

What impossible request do you have for our Lord Jesus?

Write out and read aloud Exodus 3:14.

I am who I am

God is the great I AM. This means that He is all that you need Him to be. God is saying to you, "Child I AM who I am. You fill in what you need. Do you need strength? I AM strength. Do you need power? I AM power! Do you need wisdom? deliverance? love? peace? joy? grace? mercy? loving-kindness? freedom? I AM everything that you need.

What do you need God to be for you today? Why don't you write a personal prayer to Him below and talk to your Father about your needs. He will answer your prayer.

Thank you, Jesus!

Read Titus 3:3-8 and fill in the blanks.
(3-4)
At one time we too were __________, __________, __________, and __________ by all kinds of __________ and __________. We lived in __________ and __________, being __________ and hating one another. But when the __________ and __________ of God our __________ appeared, he __________ us not because of __________ things we had done, but because of His __________.

What does Romans 2:4 say about the kindness of God?

His kindness leads us to repentance. What does that mean to you personally? Can you reflect back on the kindness of God in your life?

List the dance steps:
1.
2.
3.
4.
5.
6.
7.

Which dance step do you need more practice on?

Close in prayer.

Chapter Seven

The Family Business

The God of our fathers has chosen you to know his will and see the Righteous One and to hear the words of his mouth. You will be his witness to all men of what you have seen and heard. And now what are you waiting for? Get up, be baptized and wash your sins away, calling on his name.
(Acts 22:14-16)

The other day my little Brittany and I went for a dip at our neighborhood pool. We were loaded up with our lotion, goggles, towels and floats. I was excited to soak up the sun and read my summer book. (I don't get out much) I hadn't quite unloaded our beach bag when I noticed that Brittany had made a friend and left me...alone. (Dreams do come true.)

I watched her "yap" with our lifeguard for what seemed to be an hour. I kept saying to myself, "What is she doing?" Her little mouth was going, going, going! (Yes, like the energizer bunny!) What could they possibly be talking about? Should I go and save him? Should I rescue him from her babbling? She has such a motor mouth that my husband and I have to ask her at times to give us a "moment of silence."

I felt embarrassed. She was probably telling him everything she knew. That scared me. I could hear her telling him story after story after story. She is a people person. I am sure Brittany spreads much joy and happiness with her spunk. However, eight-year-olds never get all the information correct. I'll never forget the time when our "new neighbors" were unloading their moving trucks and their seven year old came over to introduce herself. She then let us know that her Uncle Harold made money in his basement and her father worked for a bank. Do you get the point? Children love to talk and do it with total confidence. They believe in what they are saying. My little friend Jesse told me today that her dad eats crickets. I believe her.

Then it hit me! Why am I trying to change Brittany? She's the one with the gifts. Everyone should be more like her! I need to be more like her! I was on the other side of the pool hiding my "too many Bojangle biscuits" legs under a towel. Brittany was doing what she does best spreading joy. I should have been spreading some of Jesus' joy and happiness. What kind of Bride is He returning for? One who just sits and waits or one who makes His dreams come true?

Brittany would have told that lifeguard the Gospel of Jesus Christ with full confidence and persistence. I tend to be more cautious as to who I approach. Does the Bible tell us to be cautious of about who we tell the Gospel to? Have you ever seen a flashing yellow light when you are with non-believers? The Gospel of Jesus Christ is for the whole world! The Family Business is to save souls and has been for years. Why are adults so scared to present to people the one gift that means anything? It is the one thing that our Bridegroom has asked us to do while He is away. We are to be confident that Jesus does all the work, all we have to do is be obedient to the Spirit's leading.

And yes, this lifeguard did need to be saved. He needed to be saved from this evil world and brought to the knowledge of Christ. He needed to hear story after story after story of Jesus' redeeming love. He needed to know the joy of knowing Christ. He could have even been baptized right there in the pool! As children of God, we will never know what that person you are witnessing to needs to hear. Only God knows that information. We are just to speak with His leading with confidence as His children. Hopefully, one day that lifeguard will remember a little girl who mentioned Jesus to him. Prayerfully, one day he will become a real lifesaver. Talk on, Brittany. Spread a little "Sonshine"! That is the Family Business!

Well Digging

In chapter two and three, we discovered that Abraham and Issac were a picture of God and Jesus as the Father and the Bridegroom. Let's take a quick look at how they are similar in the family business. Abraham's family business was well digging. Isaac inherited this business from his father. Jesus has inherited all from His Father. *The Father loves the loves the Son and has placed everything in his hands*. (John 3:35)

Wells in ancient times were so very important for life. Because of the hot climate a reliable water supply was essential. When a good supply of water was found a city would develop around it. *Jesus answered, "Everyone who drinks this water will be thirsty again, but whoever drinks the water I give them will never thirst. Indeed the water I give him will become in him a spring of water welling up to eternal life.* (John 4:13-14)

Water here stands for life. More specifically Jesus' life. We are to allow Jesus to dig our old self out and let Him fill us with the living water, Himself. *Therefore, if anyone is in Christ, he is a new creation; the old has gone, the new has come!* (2 Corinthians 5:17) We are then to submit to His leading to be a vessel for His glory. We are to be wells for others to draw from. We are to encourage each other to drink from the well of life. In the ancient world one held the title deed to any well they dug. Who holds the title deed to your well?

One Body, Many Parts

The body is a unit, though it is made up of many parts; and though all its parts are many, they form one body-whether Jews or Greeks, slave or free-and we were all given the one Spirit to drink. (1 Corinthians 12:12-13)

God, the Father provides for you a spiritual family of your own to mirror Himself. It consists of mothers, fathers, husbands, wives, college-buddies, childhood friends, best friends, neighbors, pastors, sisters, brothers, teachers, children, even strangers. He uses empty vessels filled with the living water to fill your every need. He sovereignly places every yielded vessel in your path. These people could be with you for a second, minute, day, years or your whole life. Only God knows how long you need her or him. You are drawn to these people because of their God-given gifts. They use their gifts to glorify God by servicing the body of Christ. Every vessel is filled with the living water and is ready for you to look into his or her well and see the reflection of Jesus. That's part of the family business. Let me give you some examples:

Splashes of Love and Commitment

My husband is my " Little Jesus." He has made a decision to serve our family with an amazing unselfish love. I feel so secure with his commitment to our family. His attitude is very contagious. I'll watch him in action and ask myself, "What does it feel like to be unselfish and totally committed to others?" I am drawn to his qualities. I recognize his characteristics as ones only God could have pour into him.

So, I go to his well and draw out an endless amount of unselfishness. He has shown me a part of Christ that I have never known before. There isn't any way anyone could be selfish around him. That has been a huge challenge for me. The credentials that he has for helping run the family business mirror Christ's unselfish love and protection. Thank you Jesus! *Honor one another above yourself.* (Romans 12:10) *Love is patient, love is kind. It does not envy, it does not boast, it is not proud. It is not rude, it is not self-seeking, it is not easily angered, it keeps no record of wrongs. Love does not delight in evil but rejoices with the truth. It always protects, always trusts, always hopes, always preservers.* (1 Corinthians 13: 4-7)

Splashes of Pastoring and Leadership

My pastor, Dr. Joe Brown is the spiritual authority at our church. He feeds his flock by being obedient to the Spirit's leading in carrying out the commands of Jesus and teaching His Word. I tell everyone that he is so anointed by God that if he told me from the pulpit how to make a peanut butter and jelly sandwich, I would listen. That sandwich would be divine. Dr. Brown's congregation drinks from his well with a thirst and a trust that God has given them.

I hope you have that kind of Pastor, leader or teacher. If you do not, that is a position in the your family business which is open. You should pray for that "job opening" to be filled. (Filled with the Living Water!) There is nothing more valuable than a Pastor after God's own heart.

God's heart is full of love for His children. Pastors reflect that love from their well to the flock. I find it very interesting that sheep are born afraid of water. It takes the shepherd being faithful and diligent to teach his sheep that water is essential to their life and the best thing for them. The Son glistens from Dr. Brown's well water. Thank you, Jesus! *His master replied, "Well done, good and faithful servant! You have been faithful with a few; I will put you in charge of many things. Come share your master's happiness!"* (Matthew 25:23)

Splashes of Wisdom, Knowledge and Motherhood

My mother is my gift of wisdom and knowledge. I can always count on her well to be full of Godly advice and counsel. I look forward to running to her well. Sometimes I get just what I want to hear. Other times, I hear the exact opposite. However, time has proven to me that whatever her advice is, it is wise that I listen. She always reminds me to seek the Lord in all things, because that is what she does.

My mother holds another very high position in my life for the Lord. She is my prayer warrior. Her prayers have covered me through many terrible days. Her prayers have covered me through many God-filled days. I'll never know all that her faithful prayers have done. Her answered prayers consist of my salvation, my personal relationship with Jesus, my wonderful husband, my beautiful children, and my ministry. I would say that she has been in the throne room quite a bit! I love you, mom! Thank you, Jesus! *Her children rise up and call her blessed!* (Proverbs 30:28)

Splashes of Loyalty

My sister Beth is my gift of loyalty and laughter. If I were to rob a bank she would blame the bank for having money. I wish you all had a sister like mine. The three gifts of love, loyalty and laughter will get you through just about anything. (My husband loves to laugh at our phone bills) My sister and I have a motto, "We may be dysfunctional, but we family!" I feel special just being her sister. You can imagine how I feel being called her friend. Thank you, Jesus! *I thank my God every time I remember you.* (Philippians 1:3)

Splashes of Tenderness and Kindness

My best friend Irene is my gift of tenderness. She will send me tenderness in the form of a card with two friends hugging or a bowl of banana pudding I mentioned I was craving. She will teach me how to make an apple pie for my first thanksgiving dinner. She will pick up my little girl with a fake tummy ache from school or she will pray for me while I am teaching a class. I have felt Christ's love from her hand.

Jesus has great surprises for you when you serve like she does. He is overflowing with such joy when he watches servanthood. There is so much joy coming from Him that he has to splash down some from His throne in heaven to the server. Watch out, Irene! Thank you, Jesus! *A gift opens the way for the giver and ushers him into the presence of the great.* (Proverbs 18:16)

Splashes of Encouragement

My friend Lee Ann is my gift of encouragement. She has been a great support throughout writing this book. I will never forget the time when the computer file for this book was missing due to "an unrecoverable disk error." (I will never forget those words as long as I live!) She tells me that I was "pitiful" when I told her. She arranged for her computer genius husband, Mark to recover the unrecoverable.

She then brought over a box of chocolate kisses for "encouragement." She described them as "kisses from Daddy." She told me that she could never make up something so sweet and she was glad that God had given her the idea. I can honestly say that "pitiful" time was well worth that splash of encouragement! Thank you, Jesus! *May the God who gives endurance and encouragement give you a spirit of unity among yourselves as you follow Christ Jesus, so that with one heart and mouth you may glorify the God and Father of our Lord Jesus Christ.* (Romans 15:5-6)

Splashes of Mentoring

My pastor's wife Teresa is my gift of mentoring. I was drawn by the Holy Spirit to her. She was living a life of dancing with Daddy when I wasn't. She was resting in Him, taking His lead, listening to His voice and talking to Him. I wanted that happiness. She had been dancing with Daddy for so long that she knew His steps. So, when He stepped toward me she took His lead and placed me in His arms. Would you like this Dance? Thank you, Jesus! *Many women do noble things, but your surpass them all.* (Proverbs 31:29)

Splashes of compassion

Our friend Frank is my gift of compassion. He is a Pastor at our church with the true spiritual gift of pastoring. If my family ever needed to go to the compassionate arms of Jesus we would run to Frank. In my opinion the gift of compassion is the hardest gift to have. When someone cries in your well-water there are ripples. That means your heart hurts as well. A heavy compassionate heart is tough to carry unless you give it to Jesus. Frank is always giving to Jesus. Thank you Jesus! *Therefore, as God's chosen people, holy and dearly loved, clothe yourselves with compassion, kindness, humility, gentleness and patience.* (Colossians 3:12)

What does it feel like to be around kind, considerate, and compassionate people? What does it feel like to receive godly wisdom and advice? What does it feel like to be encouraged and mentored in God's love? What does it feel like to be loved, encouraged and secure? It feels like dancing in God's arms. *Thank you, Jesus!*

Gospel, Inc.

God made salvation available to all through the atoning sacrifice of His Son. In order for a person to receive salvation he must first hear the testimony of Jesus Christ. Each person must be introduced personally to the Word of God. The family business is not only to mirror Jesus but to also spread the gospel of Jesus Christ to the world. We are to receive the living water and use it for the glory of God to feed and equip the Church. We are to accept the grace and spiritual gifts that God has given us to serve Him and play an active role in His plan for the redemption of the world.

Are you an ambassador for Christ? Faithful witnesses will be rewarded in heaven. I believe the greatest reward will be to see those to whom you witnessed in heaven. Doesn't that sound wonderful? There is one major difference between our family business and others: our valuable commodity is FREE! Place them in the arms of Jesus and give them the free gift of life!

Sept meet.

Chapter Seven Study Questions

Before you begin pray for wisdom and discernment needed to study His Holy Word!

List some of the people God has provided for you to mirror Jesus. Thank God in a special way for them.

family friends

What are some of the gifts that we receive from the Spirit? (Galatians 5:22-23, Romans 12, 1 Corinthians 12:1-11)

fruit of the Spirit   spiritual gift   gift of the spirit

Which gifts are you using to glorify Him?

teaching & ministry

Read 1 Corinthians 12:12-31. Write out verse18.

God has set the members.

Who has given you your spiritual gifts?

God

Read aloud and write out 1 Corinthians 12:26.

If one member suffers - all members suffer

The church is the body of Christ. Each person has their own spiritual gifts and responsibilities. We are all one body.

You are part of me and I am part of you. We are both of the same spirit. We are one in Christ Jesus. We are to encourage each other in Christ. We are to be kept accountable to each other. We are to hold each other up as we battle the enemy and prepare of Jesus' return!

Read Exodus 17:8-15.

Write out verse 12 Aaron & Hur suppated his hands

Who are your Aaron and Hur? (Hint, One of them is Jesus!)

We all have to have Aaron's in our lives. We cannot be dragged down. We have to be built up!

What happened to Joshua because of this teamwork? (verse 13) he defeated the enemy

Write out Mark 9:41. Whoever gives you a cup of water in my name, will not lose his reward.

Write out and read aloud John 7:37-38

living water will flow from your heart

Are streams of living water flowing from your mouth?

There is a condition in coming to the well and drinking. Read Isaiah 55:1 for the answer.

You have to be thirsty.

You have to be thirsty!

Let's look at Exodus 17. Read 1-7

Read verse 3 again. What were they afraid of?

They were afraid of dying w/no water.

What did God provide for them in verse 6?

water

Read Psalm 19:14.

Who is your rock?

Lord

Is that where your living water comes from?

Yes

Read Luke 16:19-31. What did the rich man ask for in verse 24?

water

Did you notice that the rich man was never given a name. However, the child of God, Lazarus, does. Read Revelation 21:27 Luke 10:19-20 for the reason why.

Only the names of the children of God are written in heaven

Those who drink of the living water have their names written in the Lambs Book of Life!
What did God say to Moses in Exodus 33:17.

He knew Moses by name

Read Revelation 21:6 and fill in the blanks.

He said to me: "It is done, I am the Alpha and the Omega, the Beginning and the End. To him who is thirsty I will give to drink without cost from the fountain of the water of life,

Write out and read aloud Revelation 7:17

lead us to living water

Where is the Lamb of God?

In heaven

Where will He lead His sheep?

to living water

Read Ephesians 5:26 and answer the following questions.

Why did Christ die for the church according to verse 26?

to sanctify & cleanse

Then how will the church be presented to Jesus on that day? (verse 27)

glorious

Read Jeremiah 2:13. What were the two sins committed?

forsaken Christ / tried their own wells

To prepare yourself for an eternity with Jesus you must drink of the Living Water, wash yourself clean with the Word of God and let others drink from your well water!

Write out Isaiah 12:3.

With joy you will draw water from the wells of salvation.

Close in prayer.

Chapter Eight

Suffering Avenue

My comfort in my suffering is this:
Your promise preserves my life.
(Psalm 119:50)

Do you know what it feels like to have true peace and joy in your life? Can you explain to me what it feels like? Can you describe it in colorful expressive words? I can imagine that it would be easier for you to describe the exact opposite, turmoil and pain. Do you know such words as tears, heartaches, sleepless nights, depression, and emptiness? Sure you do! The reason why I know that is because in order to get to true peace and joy you have to take the road directly in front of you... suffering. You cannot get to the road of peace and joy without getting to "Suffering Avenue" first.

That does not sound like very much fun, does it? You are saying, "Thanks a lot, Sheila! I was depending on this book to encourage me!" Okay then, just to keep you reading let me tell you something more important than that. You are destined to get to peace and joy! You will arrive there! Suffering is the only way to *true* peace and joy. Therefore, you must travel the roads. As Christians we are called to suffer. Yes, I said, it we are called to suffering. Just as sure as we are called to the kingdom of God we are called to suffer.

You are saying to yourself, "But, Sheila, I am a Christian. I have been forgiven for my sins and I have been reconciled back to God. There is a special covering over me that shields me from the wicked world. Suffering is from sin. I am righteous in God's sight. I am equipped with the armor you taught me about in Chapter Four!"

My reply to that is, "I am so proud of you for being grounded in truth. You are confident about your position in Christ and I am so excited for you!" However, the truth is you are not excluded from suffering. Even God's children will suffer.

I will venture to say something a little radical here: Profess to God that you are willing to suffer. Why do I say that? God uses suffering saints. You get to know God better through suffering. A.W. Tozer says," It is doubtful God can use any man greatly until He has hurt him deeply."

You will have to look at the story of Job a little deeper to find the true nugget of wisdom for the most famous Christian riddle of all times....Why do the righteous suffer?

It's hard to read the Gospel of John and the Book of Job in the same day! That is why I am glad that the apostle Paul explained Christian growth in his letters to the different churches. I am happy that God preserved the ancient letters for us to learn from today. The apostle Paul says to the church in Corinth, *Brothers, I could not address you as spiritual but as worldly-mere infants in Christ. I gave you milk, not solid food, for you were not yet ready for it.* (1 Corinthians 3:1-2) It is God, in His sovereign timing that reveals Spiritual truths to us. You are now ready to take the solid food God is ready to feed you in this lesson on suffering. Every step down Suffering Avenue gets you closer to peace and joy, so let's keep going. Are you ready? God thinks so.

Poor Job

Did you know that the Book of Job is considered to be a book of poetry like the Psalms and Proverbs? Hard to believe, isn't it? What is so poetic about suffering and trials? I was a little surprised myself the first time I read this book. I mean, God did give permission to mean ol' Satan to bring suffering and trials upon poor ol' Job!

Let's learn a little more here about poor ol' Job in verses 1:6-8. *One day the angels came to present themselves before the Lord, and Satan also came with them. The Lord said to Satan, "Where have you come from?" Satan answered the Lord, "From roaming through the earth and going back and forth in it." Then the Lord said to Satan, "Have you considered my servant Job? There is no one on earth like him; he is blameless and upright, a man who fears God and shuns evil."*

Well, there is a lot to chew on! First, let's look at the way our precious Father describes Job. He calls him blameless, upright, God-fearing and shuns evil. WOW! What a tribute! However, that is not the most fascinating part. Did you read what I read? Daddy proudly announces, "There is no one on earth like him!"

God was very proud of Job. However, Satan was given permission to touch him. Let's read Satan petitioning God in Job1: 9-12. *"Does Job fear God for nothing?" Satan replied. "Have you not put a hedge around him and his household and everything he has? You have blessed the work of his hands, so that his flocks and herds are spread throughout the land. But stretch out your hand and strike everything he has, and he will surely curse you to your face." The LORD said to Satan, "Very well, then, everything he has is in your hands, but on the man himself do not lay a finger."*

Job was torn apart at all angles. He lost his material possessions, his children and later his health. He was called to suffer. Why? What did this life lesson do for Job? What good comes out of suffering? One simple statement from Job says it all, *I know that my Redeemer lives, and that in the end he will stand upon the earth. And after my skin has been destroyed, yet in my flesh I will see God, I myself will see him with my own eyes-I and not another. How my heart yearns within me!* (Job 19: 25-27) This is a powerful testimony from Job. He tells us that after all sufferings there is only one true thing. A Redeemer lives and he is coming back. It is called our blessed hope. *While we wait for the blessed hope-the glorious appearing of our great God and Savior, Jesus Christ, who gave himself for us to redeem us from all wickedness and to purify for himself a people that are his very own, eager to do what is good.* (Titus 2:13-14) Your husband may have left you, Jesus will not. Your children may have left you in pain, Jesus will comfort you. You may have lost everything you own, but you have Jesus! Someone you love may have crushed your spirit, Jesus will mend you. He is the *one true thing*! I promise on His promises!

Faith In Suffering

We may never know all of the answers to why we suffer until we are with Jesus in eternity. However, we do not suffer without the blessed hope that at the end of our road is Jesus. Let's read some of that verse again, *I will see him with my own eyes-I and not another…* (Job 19:26) Job knew that he would see his Savior in the flesh. That is where he placed his hope during suffering.

When you are suffering, no one is going to have to tell you Jesus is near you. You will feel and see Him for yourself. You can feel Him right beside you. He is your *personal* Savior. He lives right in *your* heart. *I pray that out of his glorious riches he may strengthen you with power through his Spirit in your inner being, so that Christ may dwell in your hearts through faith.* (Ephesians 3:16-17) Do not miss something important here. Did you read the part where Christ dwells in our hearts through faith? It all starts with faith. Faith in Him starts the music to your dance. You do not have to wait for Him to return for you to dance with Him. Reach for His hand now. Have that kind of faith and the song will start!

If it takes suffering for you to reach for Jesus it will be allowed. God will do what it takes to get you to perfect peace, love and joy. The suffering may bring you to Jesus for the first time or it may bring you to more of Jesus. Whatever the case, you will yearn for Him. *How my heart yearns within me!* (Job 19:27) It is in the arms of Jesus where you start your dance. In His arms you will find all you need. Don't ever regret any day of suffering allowed by God. Your dance will have the magnificent splendor of grace and dignity when you are taking His lead. You will not want to miss a step!

A Transforming Love

Let us not forget that it cost the Son of God a life of humility, suffering and death to reconcile us to God. *But you see Jesus, who was made a little lower than angels, now crowned with glory and honor because he suffered death, so that by the grace of God he might taste death for everyone.* (Hebrews 2:9) Next, came the almighty power of God in the resurrection and ascension of Jesus. *I want to know Christ and the power of His resurrection and the fellowship of sharing in his sufferings, becoming like Him in death, and so somehow, to attain to the resurrection from the dead.* (Philippians 3:10) Jesus is now at the right hand of the Father, where He is glorified. *But when this priest had offered for all time one sac-*

rifice for sins, he sat down at the right hand of God." (Hebrews 10:12) The same happens to us when we endure suffering for God's sake. We suffer. We endure. We die to self. We become one with Jesus. The power of God flows and the Son of God is glorified! It is the transforming power of God's love that will restore you through this difficult process.

To experience Jesus' transforming love you have to *allow* Him to restore you, satisfy you, but most of all you have to let Him love you. Can you think for a second about doing that for Him? You need to turn the tables of love and refresh Him, satisfy Him and most of all love Him. Have you ever had a relationship where you did all the work? It's not very rewarding is it? It eventually will fade into a small amount of existence. However, if you took time to know that person and what they loved in a relationship, what satisfies them, what restores them and show them that they are truly loved, you have a relationship. You *need* a relationship with Jesus. Resting in Jesus during suffering brings forth a very intimate one. Your part in this relationship is resting and dancing.

Overcoming

I categorize suffering in two ways. One is the suffering from sin in the world. For example, divorce, abuse, death, disease, and many other forms of pain. You fill in the blanks. This kind of suffering breaks the heart of God. He cannot bear the pain of watching you go through it. The way He is comforted is by you running to *His* arms for comfort! Second is suffering to conquer the flesh. Let's take a look at Job again. Job knew he was being tested. But for what? *But he knows the way I take; when he tested me, I will come forth as gold.* (Job 23:10) Saints are allowed to suffer so that they may see their true selves. Why? Let's go back to the Scripture in Titus 2:13-14. *While we wait for the blessed hope-the glorious appearing of our great God and Savior, Jesus Christ, who gave himself for us to redeem us from all wickedness and to purify for himself a people that are his very own, eager to do good.* That scripture tells us Jesus died for our sins *and* to purify us to be His own. Remember Jesus is pursuing a bride that is holy, spotless and blameless. A holy bride is His work in progress right now. The Spirit is pursuing that daily. An example of this kind of suffering might be a Christian who is prideful. Jesus cannot have a prideful bride. Pride is not from Him. Humility is. Therefore, that part of the flesh, pride, has to be dealt with and replaced. God will reveal that character by testing through allowed suffering. Once character is revealed and *detested* it will be replaced. The result is becoming the *perfectly compatible bride* Jesus is praying for.

There may be pain and humiliation along the way to overcoming flesh however; it will be worth it. What is more important than you becoming a prepared bride for the Son? His life in you is an everlasting treasure. That treasure is eternal and stored in heaven for a grand purpose. It is the most precious gift you could give Jesus, the gift of you. The gift of a holy you is the wedding gift that he is waiting for. An eternal gift to be opened in heaven to start eternity together.

You must overcome self! What does overcome mean? It is overcoming your sinful flesh and replacing it with the abundance of Jesus. That sounds impossible, doesn't it? Well it is not. Jesus has overcome so you can overcome through Him. *To him who overcomes, I will give the right to sit with me on my throne, just as I overcame and sat down with my Father on his throne. Revelation 3:21.* You may go into a circumstance of humiliation however, your responsibility is to come out of it righteously. You may then meet the character of Christ that you didn't know before! Amen to that!

Rest

Resting in Him during suffering is very critical for your spiritual growth. *Come to me, all who are weary and burdened, and I will give you rest. Take my yoke upon you and learn from me, for I am gentle and humble in heart and you will find rest for your souls. For my yoke is easy and my burden is light.* (Matthew 11:28) I am always working up a plan to straighten out my life's problems. I get busy doing this, that and everything I can to put my plan into action. I think I have to keep busy! Do something! Then God lovingly will remind me that Jesus, our high priest, is not standing anymore in the Holy of Holies working. His work is complete. It is finished! He is sitting right beside the Father. (In a position of royalty, I might add!) He reminds me to rest and let Jesus, who has already conquered all, take over *my action plan*. In other words, he tells me to *sit down*! Rest!

You must be weak for Him to be strong! *But he said to me, "My grace is sufficient for you, for my power is made perfect in weakness." Therefore I will boast all the more gladly about my weaknesses, so that Christ's power may rest on me. That is why, for Christ's sake, I delight in weaknesses, insults, in hardships, in persecutions, in difficulties. For when I am weak, then I am strong.* (2 Corinthians 12:9-10) He will sustain you. *Cast your cares on the LORD and he will sustain you; he will never let the righteous fall.* (Psalm 55:22) His compassion and mercies are new each day. *The Lord's great love we are not consumed, for his compassions never fail. They are new every morning; great is your faithfulness.* (Lamentations 3:22-23) Great is His faithfulness.

Did you notice in the verse above, 2 Corinthians 12:9-10 that Christ's power rests on you when you are weak. Thank the Lord! Rest in the original Greek means to *abide with*. The power of His Spirit will abide with you when you are weak. When you yield yourself to Him you are not weak but powerful. You have the power to conquer pride, conceit, selfishness, stinginess or any other characteristic from your old self. More of Him, less of you! The more you dance with Him the more you are like Him! That's when the dance is electrifying.

Knock, Knock

In times of suffering you *will* cry out for Jesus' love. In the process of His unbelievable healing you will be anxious to return that love to Him. Don't forget you do that by giving Him more of yourself. We are to die to self daily. *If anyone would come after me, he must deny himself and take up his cross daily and follow me. For whoever wants to save his life will lose it, but whoever loses his life for me will save it.* (Luke 9:23-24) You usually do not notice that you are holding on to self until you open the door of suffering. You see, if you were truly dead to self you wouldn't be hit so hard when suffering knocks. You would have let Jesus answer the door.

You Really Love Me!

When my husband and I were dating he went to great lengths to let me know that he loved me. I was away from him one summer. He decided to come and surprise me with a visit. He gave up a shift at work and drove for seven hours to be with me for only four hours. When I saw him and realized what he had done I said, " You must really love me!" It was a great feeling. I remember it to this day. There is no greater feeling than to have the security of someone's love.

When I endure pain and suffering because I know I have to for an eternal purpose, I close my teary eyes and tilt my face toward heaven for comfort. I can then hear Jesus say, "You are enduring for me! You must really love me!" My reply, " I do." Those are the wedding vows that we have to keep every day to Him. "I do" to His will. "I do" to his character. Those vows take work!

You never ever have to worry about Jesus' faithfulness to you. *Give thanks to the Lord, for he is good; his love endures forever.* (1 Chronicles 16:34) He never changes. It is you who needs to be faithful. How? Praying in the throne room. Worshipping in the throne room. Praising in the throne room. Submitting in the throne room. Growing spiritually in the throne room. That is when you become one with Him in perfect harmony. The throne room is where your relationship flourishes. Spending time there with your Savior is where intimacy begins. Trust me He will meet you anywhere. But, eventually He will point your eyes to the magnificent throne room where love and miracles pour out abundantly! You need to be there. It's on the *throne room floor* that you learn to *dance*.

You Have Arrived at Peace and Joy!

One way Webster's Dictionary describes a road is *any way of advancing and progressing*. What will taking the road of suffering advance you to? The arms of Jesus! Your road might be long and bumpy. You may be stretched as far as you can bear it and broken beyond belief. But it is there that you will find Jesus. It is much better to be in the wilderness with Jesus for an eternal purpose than without Him in your own promised land!

Jesus' arms were stretched as far as they could go and nailed to a cross for you. They are now stretched out as far as they can go for you to run to. He died because he does not want to be without you. He knew the road He had to take before *you* could reach *true* peace and joy. He took

"Suffering Avenue." By taking that road He made a way for peace between you and the Father. By taking that road He made a way for joy between you and Him. Your relationship with Jesus is the eternal treasure that angels marvel to see! Find your peace and joy in that my friend. Now run to the arms of Jesus and practice your dancing!

Chapter Eight Study Questions

Before you begin pray for the wisdom and discernment needed to study His Holy Word!

Read Hebrews 2:9-10 and fill in the blanks.

But we see Jesus, who was made a little lower than the angels, now ________ with ________ and ________ because he ________ death, so that by the ________ of God he might taste ________ for everyone.

In bringing many sons to ________, it was fitting that God, for whom and through whom everything ________, should make the ________ of their salvation ________ through ________

Salvation is made perfect through what?

How do we know that suffering is required for obedience? (Hebrews 5:8-9)

Write out Romans 8:17-18

What are we to share with Christ along with His suffering?

Read in John 15:1-2. What does pruning (suffering) produce?

We are called to suffer and to share in His glory. Our salvation is made perfect through suffering. We learn obedience through suffering. We mature through suffering. Our fruits increase when we suffer. Suffering is a friend.

Pray with me from Psalm 139:23-24 and ask God to reveal to us what we can learn from Him today through our friend, suffering.

Father,
Search me, O God and know my heart;
Test me and know my anxious thoughts.
See if there is any offensive way in me,
And lead me in the way of the everlasting.
In Jesus' name, Amen

Read Isaiah 61:1-7 and fill in the blanks.
(1-3)
The Spirit of the __________ Lord is on me, because the Lord has __________ me to preach __________ to the poor. He has sent me to bind up the __________, to proclaim __________ for the __________ and release from __________ for the prisoners, to proclaim the year of the Lord's __________ and the day of vengeance of our God, to __________ all who mourn, and __________ for those who grieve in Zion- to bestow on them a __________ of ______ instead of __________, the oil of __________ instead of __________ and a garment of __________ instead of a spirit of __________. They will be called oaks of __________, a planting of the Lord for the display of His __________.

God can *bind up* your *broken heart*! God can proclaim *freedom* for you and release you from darkness! This is the year of the Lord's *favor*! He will *comfort* your mourning with *gladness* and you will *praise* Him! He will provide for you during your grieving by replacing your ashes with a *crown of beauty*!

We will become "oaks of righteousness". What does Isaiah 51:8 say about righteousness?

It will be forever!

Read 1 Peter 5:10 and fill in the blanks

And the God of all grace, who called __us__ to His eternal __glory__ in __Christ__, after you have __suffered__ a little while, will ________ ________ you and make you ________, ______ and ________.

What will God do for you after suffering?

settle us

Suffering is for a little while and righteousness is forever.

Read Isaiah 32:17.

What is the fruit of righteousness? peace

What will the effect of righteousness be?

quietness & assurance forever

There is peace through suffering for righteousness!

Read Isaiah 30:15 and fill in the blanks

"In __returning__ and __rest__ is your __salvation__,
In __quietness__ and __confidence__ is your __strength__

Go back to Isaiah 61:7 and fill in the blanks.

Instead of their shame my people will receive a double portion, and instead of [illegible] they will rejoice in their [illegible]; and so they will inherit a double portion in their land, and everlasting joy will be theirs!

What will be everlasting? joy

What was Jesus anointed with in Hebrews 1:9?

oil of gladness

Why? Look at Hebrews 12:2.

joy

What was the joy set before Him? right side of the throne

The answer is you! You were the joy set before Jesus! You see Jesus knows what awaits you in eternity and His life was worth you having it! He loves you that much! Find you joy in that my precious friend!

In John 17:13 you will find something Jesus prayed for. What is it? having joy

He prayed for you to have His own joy, divine joy! Do you?

Read John 15:9-11 and answer the following questions.

Who does Jesus compare His love to you to?

His Fathers love

How do you remain in Jesus' love?

by keeping His commandments

How has Jesus remained in the Father's love?

by keeping His Father's commandments

What was Jesus' reason for telling you this?

that our joy may be full

Truth was given for you to have joy! Hunt for it like a treasure!

Write out 1 John 2:5. Whoever keeps His word - abides in Him.

Jesus loves you the same as He loves the Father. For you to love Jesus that much you must first obey His commandments. That is when your joy will be made complete. Obeying His Holy Word also brings about peace, love, strength, wisdom, tenderness and compassion. I believe that is a fair trade!

Look at something interesting in Luke 10:21.

Where was Jesus getting His joy?

from His Father

Write out Galatians 5:22. The fruits of the Spirit

Write out and read aloud Psalm 16:11. Where is true joy found? in His presence

Joy is found in His presence.

How is God described in Psalm 43:4? Is that how you would describe Him? my exceeding joy

Read 1 Chronicles 16:27. What else do we find in the God's presence? honor, majesty, strength, gladness

Write out Nehemiah 8:10. How are joy and strength related? the joy of the Lord is our strength.

List the three commands given in 1 Thessalonians 5:16.

1. rejoice always

2. pray w/out ceasing

3. give thanks in all

This is God's will for you!

Read Matthew 11:28 and fill in the blanks:

Come to __me__, all you who are __heavy-laden__ and __weary / labor__, and I will give you __rest__. Take on my __yoke__ upon you and learn from me, for I am __gentle__ and __lowly__ in heart, and you will find __rest__ for your souls.

What are you promised in this verse?

rest

Your resting during suffering obligates Him to give you His peace and joy! Don't miss this wonderful opportunity to rest with your Savior.

Read Psalm 30:5.

Read John 16:33 and fill in the blanks.

I have told you these things, so that __in__ __me__ you may have __peace__. In this __world__ you will have __tribulation__. But take heart! I have __overcome__ the __world__.

Write out 2 Thessalonians 3:16!

May the Lord of peace – give you His peace!

Close in prayer.

Chapter Nine

A Closer Waltz with Jesus

"Because He loves me," says the Lord, "I will rescue him;
I will protect him, for he acknowledges my name.
He will call upon me, and I will answer him;
I will be with him in trouble.
I will deliver him and honor him.
(Psalm 91:14-15)

Sitting down to start this chapter brought tears to my eyes. We are at the end of our journey. Tears can have many different meanings. My tears are representing every type of emotion possible: joy, happiness, sadness, grieving and liberation. As I have shared with you in the introduction, I was called to *live and relive* all chapters in this book. Unbelievably to me, God kept this chapter on grace, love, and mercy last on His agenda.

Little did I know that the first person whom this book would help would be me. My precious pastor's wife has been wise in her words, " God cannot let you teach others by you just knowing the truth. You have to live it." There is an extraordinary difference in knowing the truth and living the truth. Do you want to live the truth no matter what the cost? If so, count on a whole lot of pain, suffering, and surprises overpowered by God's grace, love and mercy. (That was supposed to be an encouraging sentence!)

For some strange reason, I feel like I am "on my own" in this chapter. By that, I mean that I feel God's presence and anointing, but I am to "testify" myself of His grace, love, and mercy. I am to testify of all that He has done for me. I am to testify to all that He wants to do and can do for you! I am to testify to what yielding to the truths revealed in this book can do for you. I pray for the words to be adequate enough.

Testifying

Let me "testify" here a little bit. I can sincerely tell you that I have recently needed to equip myself with the full armor you were taught about in chapter four. Satan hit me hard. Put the armor on, my friends! It protects you!

I have recently survived on the words of comfort given on suffering in chapter eight. Run to the arms of Jesus precious one! His arms are warm, comforting and wide open!

I have just today had to dance close to Daddy to overcome again the familiar enemies: insecurities, doubts and rejections that were portrayed in chapter one. Dance away, ladies! You will triumph over those enemies!

Lastly, I can assertively testify that I have experienced the fullness of God's grace, love, and mercy. Listen up my friends! God will shower every hurdle we jump, every cut we endure, and every sting we feel with His *grace, love and mercy*. He will give you as much as you need and then more!

The Gift of Grace

What is grace? Grace, in the New Testament Greek language is *charis*, meaning "unmerited favor." There is nothing that we can do to earn "favor" in the eyes of God. It is by the grace of God that we have anything. It is by His grace that we breathe. It is by His grace that we are allowed to serve Him. It was by His grace that we were chosen to be His. It is by His grace that we are allowed to sit in His presence. It is by His grace that we are enabled to become like Jesus! So, what is grace? Grace is the favoritism God shows His children. However, there is some responsibility on our part; we have to respond to it!

There is much more to learn about God's grace. Grace is also the supernatural blessing God gives us to face the days of failure, the hours of weakness, the minutes of frustration and inadequacy. You see grace is more than receiving undeserved gifts from God. It is also receiving God's compassion, kindheartedness, concern and care during difficult times. His grace added to our hurt, pain, and disappointment is one of the most wonderful gifts God could ever give us. It ranks right behind the gift of salvation and the gift of Holy Spirit dwelling inside us.

God's grace is undeserved. That's what makes His compassion and loving-kindness so surprising. I would think that my personal history would disqualify me as an ambassador for a holy God. I was in bondage to Satan's lies for many years. I chose to believe Satan's lies over God's truths. My human mind would respond to someone like that with an, "I told you so!" God responds to someone like that with an, "I love you so!"

Looking back, I can see that God was with me the whole time. Because of His grace I am alive today. There were many times when I believe Satan was pointing me toward the death I deserved. My addictions and bondage were torture to my mind and body. God wanted something better for me and decided to grant me grace.

God wasn't waiting at the front door for me to come back home. He walked out the front door and followed me and never left my side. He carried me back home where the aroma of sweet grace abides. We are His children and the atmosphere of His home is that of warmth and security. You know that you are "home" the minute you walk in the door.

Does He need to take you home today? He has followed you this far. He has never left your side. Can you smell the fragrance of His sweet grace? Welcome Home! Run to the arms of the Father of amazing grace. His grace carries us through and lifts us up. Oh, that sweet Grace!

Are you living under the power of grace and truth or are you bound to chains of guilt and shame? Are you accepting grace or turning from it? You need grace to run the race! You have to make this decision every day of your life!

How are we to approach the throne of grace? Hebrew 4:16 tells us to go confidently. Once you accept God's grace you then move to the next level which is, Glory! You go from *guilt* to *groaning* to *grace* to *GLORY*! What are you choosing today guilt and groaning or grace and glory?

Read what God says to those who think they are too weak to carry the heavy burden of guilt and groaning in 2 Corinthians 12:9: *My grace is sufficient for you, for my power is made perfect in weakness.* Where you are weak He is strong! Hallelujah! Praise God! Now hand your Father your guilt and groaning so that He can begin His work!

The Gift of Love

What is love? The word love used in the Bible to explain God's love is *agape. Agape* is a divine love. *For God so "agape" the world that he gave his one and only Son, that whoever believes in him shall not perish but have eternal life.* (John 3:16) This love is affectionate, yet its basis is always on what is best and right for you. Only God can bestow this kind of love. We can provide this type of love to others only through the manifestation of the Holy Spirit.

The one thing that every person on this earth is looking for is love. Love seems to cure a whole lot of wrong. The other day my husband happened to hear the fighting going on between our two children. They were fussing over something that made them both start crying. He decided to cure the situation by tickling them both. Their crying soon turned into outrageous laughter! Their laughter made me laugh. Their laughter made my husband smile. They have no idea what they were fighting about to this day. My husband's act of love spread throughout our house and everyone felt tickled.

That night I asked God in my prayers to tickle my heart with His love. The next day, I had lunch with a friend who God used to tickle my heart with encouraging words. Another friend was used to tickle my heart with a very meaningful gift that brought tears to my eyes. Another friend took my little Stevie to see NASCAR great Jeff Gordon (that tickled this mother's heart!).

I cannot list all of the constant tickles I received that day. I wished I had of asked God to tickle me sooner! My tickles turned my most recent worries and struggles into smiles and laughter. Have you asked God to tickle your heart with His love? He will do it! God's love cures everything.

I can reflect back on many times in my life where I was in so much pain that I couldn't function. You may remember many times like that yourself. You may be living one of those times right now. I can assure you that God is anxious to take your pain away! His specialty is exchanging pain for love.

I just recently went through a cut to my heart. I couldn't seem to get past it for some reason. My heart was bleeding. I kept running to God for a "Daddy hug." He provided the comfort I needed, but I would then jump off His lap and run back to my life to see if my pain was gone.

When I would find out that I was still going through a tough time I would run back to Him. Again, He would hold me, encourage me and love me. I would spend a greater period of time with Him and then again run from the throne room back to my "life."

I would consistently find out that the pain was still there. It took me going back and forth several times, hoping that the end was near, before I just broke down in God's arms. I said, "Daddy every time I leave I get hurt again." Daddy replied, "Why don't you just stay!" *The Lord is close to the brokenhearted and saves those who are crushed in spirit.* (Psalm 34:18)

My friend, you never ever have to leave the loving arms of our Father! He is there to bind up your broken heart! You are safe in His all comforting, all powerful, everlasting love!

God's holy love is unconditional and it never changes. In spite of our condition we are loved completely and forever. I have had relationships that have changed in a minute. I have had a father who left me, friends who moved away, and babies who grew up. Not one single thing on this earth is permanent. The only thing eternal that can keep us looking forward to another tomorrow is God's love. You must eventually choose this love above all else. Nothing will satisfy you the way God's love can. *Agape* love will sustain you. *Agape* love will never leave you nor forsake you!

The Gift of Mercy

What is mercy? The Greek translation for mercy is *eleos*. *Eleos* "is the outward manifestation of pity; it assumes need on the part of him who receives it, and resources adequate to meet the need on the part of him who shows it." God is merciful to His children and we are in need of His mercies every day. Mercy is the act of compassion God gives to the sinful and troubled. Where death and punishment is deserved, God grants mercy.

But when the kindness and love of God our Savior appeared, he saved us, not because of righteous things we had done, but because of his mercy. (Titus 3:4-5) Paul tells us in Romans 12:1 that because of God's mercy we should offer ourselves as living sacrifices, holy and pleasing to God. Once a child of the King has received His mercy, he or she does not act out of duty by submitting to Him; they act out of love and devotion to the One who is worthy!

I am constantly finding out that I am falling short of what God has called me to be. There have been many times during the writing of this book that I have sinned and fell before God asking Him to forgive me and to grant me mercy. The writing of this book has not been, "The year of Saint Sheila." It has been the year of revelation and refining. I had pleaded for God not to take this calling away from me. Your holding this book in your hand is proof of His mercy. I am living proof.

Receiving Grace, Love and Mercy

Knowing that we are not worthy enough for the grace God has allowed us is why we praise His holy name. Knowing that He has deemed us worthy enough to receive His love is why we return love with all of our heart. Knowing that we are not worthy enough for the mercy handed to us is why we bow down in His presence. Grace is His favoritism toward us. His Love for us is divine. His mercies are new every day. What an awesome God we serve!

Let's talk a little bit now about our response to His gracious, loving-kindness. We are to yield as vessels, be obedient to submit all to Him and, above all, love Him enough to do it!

Yielding

I will never forget this journey labeled "yielding." Remember, when you yield you become more like Jesus. Therefore, you are capable and prepared to be used in any capacity called by God. True vessels can feel the living water being poured into them. They know the difference between living in the flesh and living in the abundance of Jesus. True vessels know that God is working a mighty work in their lives for His glory. True vessels know that this refining process is painful. True vessels, therefore, look forward to the supreme embrace of God's grace, love and mercy.

God delights in the fact that He freely gave us grace, love, and mercy when we didn't deserve it. He is ecstatic by the fact we *yearn* for His grace, mercy and love as we pursue His plan for our lives. Do you yearn to know God intimately? You can know Him! He loves you that much. Are you wondering what God's plan is for your life? Because of His grace there is one! An exciting plan! Are you praying about what character of Christ you are to pursue today? It's yours to have! Because of His mercy you are complete in Christ. Your only job is having faith enough to submit all to Him.

Submitting

We submit ourselves to Jesus understanding that He knows us better than we know ourselves. Our submission is obedience to Him. He knows what we need to endure to be ready for His return. God orchestrates our life situations to prepare us as Jesus' bride. The reality is that we truly do not even know what God is working out in our lives until the struggle is over.

There have been many times that my mouth has fallen to the floor when my flesh has been revealed to me through a certain situation. I never knew I had such reactions in me! Only Jesus could have known what I needed to acknowledge in my flesh and overcome. Remember that He exposes our weaknesses so that we can pursue the holiness He is after in His bride. It is much better to deal with it here and be ready for Him. The hurting, struggle, or humiliation on earth will be nothing compared to the glory you will share with Jesus in eternity.

Then there are those situations that have nothing to do with you, but they affect you. Other people's sin affects us. I have been utterly shocked before at a given situation. I had no idea what really hit me. I was just minding my own business when…BAM. It hit! Kind of like an unexpected bill in the mail. You didn't budget for it, you didn't ask for it and you certainly weren't ready for it (much less excited about it).

However, it is something you have to deal with. Satan will throw every hurdle he can to discourage God's children. Like Job, we must trust God, and endure until He reveals the purpose. You have to keep moving toward the throne room for the good in the matter. Why? It truly pleases Jesus that you are submitting all to Him. Submitting all means you want what He wants. Submitting all means that you trust He will work all things out for your ultimate best and for His glory. It is your submission and obedience to Him that proves your love for Him.

You should strive to be all that He has called for you to be. You were called to Him before the creation of the world. You do not want to miss pleasing the Father by not submitting all. As a Daddy's girl you are called to greatness. We cannot achieve such a high calling without the mighty hand of God carrying us through! We cannot achieve it without submitting all to that mighty hand!

True Love

We all are anxious for the return of our Bridegroom. I am constantly thinking of that day. The other day during praise and worship at my church someone blew a shofar (see chapter three) and I felt like jumping on a trampoline to rapture myself. We are all waiting for that day.

However, the church is not ready spiritually for Jesus. The bride has to make herself ready! *Let us rejoice and be glad and give him glory! For the wedding of the Lamb has come, and is bride has made herself ready.* (Revelation 19:7) In other words, God is not finished with us yet! I believe the reason the church is so weak right now is because we do not dwell in the power of His grace, love and mercy. We are an unbelieving church right now. We are not in the midst of Him. We are in the midst of our puny little selves. We may be in the outer skirts of His power, but we are not dwelling in Him. We are only camping out in the outer courts.

Let's start to move into the very presence of God. Let's capture all that is ours as the church. His Holy Spirit's presence gives us the power, wisdom and authority in Christ Jesus to pursue His will and the joy that follows! Your call in life is to be a prepared bride for Jesus. You cannot do that out of His presence. More than that, He wants us near. He desires us to be near. Dwelling in His midst keeps our tears wiped away, our chin up and our hearts mended. Who could ask for more?

Once you dwell in the presence of flawless love you can conquer all. You may be struggling with your flesh. True love is patient. You may not feel worthy of love. True love is yours to have this very minute! Your child may be a prodigal. True love always hopes. You may feel hopeless in your addiction. True love always endures. You may feel weak or even scared. True love always protects. You may not see your dreams fulfilled. True love always trusts. There are extremely hurtful situations that we all will face. However, we do not have to face them alone. *Love is patient, love is kind. It does not envy, it does not boast, it is not proud. It is not rude, it is not self-seeking, it is not easily angered, it keeps no record of wrongs. Love does not delight in evil but rejoices with the truth. It always protects, always trusts, always hopes, always perseveres.* (1Corinthians 13:4-7)

Face to Face

I am sure that you are looking forward to asking Jesus many questions. You probably have your list right in front of you labeled, "*Questions for Jesus!*" Why did my father leave us? Why did that accident have to happen? Why did my friend die so young? Why was my child born disabled? Why was I hurt so badly by the one I love and trusted? There is room here for you to fill in more blanks.

There *will* be a time when you will see Him *face to face*. *Your* first reaction upon seeing *Him* will be to bow before all of His majesty! *His* first reaction upon seeing *you* will be to hold you personally for the first time. He will be holding His dreams in His arms. You will be crying with relief from finally being with Him. He will wipe away your tears.

Then you will take a long stroll with Jesus down the streets of gold. You will then have your opportunity to ask Him questions. Your head will rest on His familiar shoulder and your hand will be in the hand that can halt all creation. He will be enthralled by your beauty and pleased that you are with Him. You will then see that smile that you live for and He will question, "Did you say that you have something you want to ask me?"

There will be nothing more important in your whole life than this moment with Jesus. You will see things so clearly. You will understand everything. Nothing will compare to belonging to Him. So, your reply will be, " No, No questions. I only want to tell you, my Jesus, that I am thankful for whatever you planned and allowed before creation to bring me to you."

Then you will take the hand that created you. You will hold the palm that has your name written on it. You will be in the arms that you have run to many times. You will dance on the feet that guide you to all truth. You will look into the eyes that watched you every second of your life. You will touch the face of love and dance down the streets of gold with your Bridegroom. There are no last dances in heaven, only eternal dances.

Chapter Nine Study Questions

Before you begin pray for the wisdom and discernment needed to study his holy word.

We are going to dig deep into some truths revealed in scripture on the magnificent grace, love and mercy of our Heavenly Father! Are you ready to never be the same again? Say good-bye to your old self… here we go!

Write out and read aloud Ephesians 2:8.

It is by grace I am saved...

Write out and read aloud Romans 3:23.

All have sinned

Write out and read aloud John 1:16.

We've all received His fullness

When God wants to make a serious point in scripture He will repeat Himself! Go read Psalm 136 and find out what God is serious about you knowing!

Read Exodus 15:13 with me:

In your unfailing love you will lead the people you redeemed.
In your strength you will guide them to your dwelling place!

Read Jeremiah 31:3-4 and fill in the blanks.

The LORD appeared to us in the past, saying:
I have lovd you with an everlasting love;
I have drawn you with loving kindness. I will build
you up again and you will be rebuilt, O virgin Israel. Again
you will take your tambourines and go out to dance
with the rejoicers.

Where are you dancing shoes?

Read Psalm 21:7. What happen to you when you trust in God's unfailing love?

we are shown his mercy

Read Psalm 33:18. What happens when you put your hope in God's unfailing love?

We have God's mercy

Now read Psalm 119:76. How is God's unfailing love described here?

as merciful kindness

Next read Psalm 6:4. Why did God save you?

for mercie's sake

Last read Psalm 13:5 and write it out.

I have trusted in your mercy

Now read with me 1 Corinthians 2:9: *No eye has seen, no ear has heard, no mind has conceived what God has prepared for those who love him.*

What command do you find in Deuteronomy 6:5?

That we love the Lord w/ all our heart, all our soul, all our strength

Write out 1 Corinthians 8:3.

He knows us.

Read Ephesians 5:1. How can we be imitators of God?

Walk in love.

Read Romans 5:5 and you will find the only way that you can give *agape* love.

by the Holy Spirit

Read Colossians 3:12-14 and fill in the blanks to verse 14:

And over all these things put on love, which binds them all together in one unity.

Read 1 Peter 4:8 with me now!

Above all, love each other deeply, because love covers over a multitude of sins.

Was I right? Are you a changed person knowing God's truth on His grace and love? Now let's move to mercy.

Read Daniel 9:9 and 18 with me.

(9) The Lord our God is merciful and forgiving, even though we have rebelled against Him. (18b) We do not make requests of you because we are righteous, but because of your great mercy.

Write out Matthew 5:7.

Blessed are the merciful

Write out Proverbs 28:13.

How do we find mercy?

by confessing our sins

Take a minute here to renounce anything that may be keeping you from God's mercy.

Read Psalm 57:1 with me.

Have mercy on me, O God, have mercy on me, for in you my soul takes refuge. I will take refuge in the shadow of your wings until the disaster has passed.

How long can you take refuge in the shadow of God's wings?

forever

God loves you and has done many things for you to know of His love. Read Mark 5:19. What command does Jesus give?

By telling others what God has done for us.

Have you done that? You are to testify of His amazing grace, love and mercy! Go tell it on the mountain!

Close in prayer.

Chapter Ten

Becoming a Prepared Bride for Jesus

If we endure, we will also reign with Him.
(2 Timothy 2:12)

My friends, Jesus loves you more than His own life. He doesn't want to be without you for one minute. Start dancing with Him this very day. Live the rest of your life getting ready for an eternity with Him. Your purpose in life is an eternal purpose. You are to spend your life glorifying the Father and preparing yourself to be His Son's bride!

I am going to suggest in this chapter some of the ways that have been revealed to me to prepare for Jesus' return. This past year, by His grace, I have yielded to this preparation. I have found the process to be very difficult. I have walked through many of these truths and stumbled on all. I have failed many times at them. I have learned the victory comes when you press on!

You must let go of any obstacles or hindrances that are keeping you from pressing on towards your Bridegroom. *Therefore, since we are surrounded by such a great cloud of witnesses, let us throw off everything that hinders and the sin that so easily entangles, and let us run with perseverance the race marked out for us.* (Hebrews 12:1) Once they are removed, never look back. Don't let them keep you from Jesus. Don't let them be a drag on you while you're striving to finishing the race. Do I need to remind you what happened to Lot's wife when she looked back? Enough said.

Refiner's Fire

I was gripped by something during the writing of this book that would not let me go. I was smothered by a powerful hold. I couldn't get out of the hand that had me. Something was keeping me from *my* destination. That something was God's love. God's powerful love will never let you go out of His refining hand.

Please understand that God knows you inside and out. There are no secrets with Him. He knows the real you. That is a scary thought isn't it? Someone knows you innermost thoughts. But it is true and praise God for it! He loves you so much that He isn't going to let you escape. Satan, sin, the world and flesh has attempted to taint Jesus' bride and God wants her purified!

Remember, the blood of Jesus cleanses us, but we also need to be purified and that is not an easy process. We are purified though the fire of suffering! *But who can endure the day of his coming? Who can stand when he appears? For he will be like a refiner's fire or a launderer's soap. He will sit as a refiner and purifier of silver; he will purify the Levites and refine them like gold and silver. Then the Lord will have men who bring offerings in righteousness.* (Malachi 3:2-4) Yes, I said it we have to go through the Refiners fire! The hot, painful, sweat-dripping, dreadful fire! Your fire is usually waiting for you in what scripture calls the wilderness.

Let's look at two scripture verses that will comfort you during the Refiner's fire. First is Song of Solomon 3:6. *Who is this coming up from the desert like a column of smoke, perfumed with myrrh and incense?* In this scripture we find out that when we are going through the fire we never come out of it smelling like smoke. No way! When we are put through the fire for an eternal purpose we come out of it smelling like myrrh and incense. In other words, we come out of it more like Jesus! There is a grand purpose in the fire.

Take a deep breath and go to the second verse, Song of Solomon 8:5. *Who is this coming up from the desert leaning on her lover?* Who is with you in the fire/wilderness? Your Bridegroom is there holding you up! Do I need to remind you of Shadrach, Meshach and Abednego? Read Daniel 3 for a refresher course. These three men were put in a fire by King Nebuchadnezzar because they refused his command to bow and worship a false God. Notice verses 24-25, *Then King Nebuchadnezzar leaped to his feet in amazement and asked his advisers, "Weren't there three men that we tied up and threw into the fire?" They replied, "Certainly, O king." He said, "Look! I see four men walking around in the fire, unbound and unharmed, and the fourth looks like a son of the gods."* Jesus is with you in the fire!

Go further to verses 26-27. *Nebuchadnezzar then approached the opening of the blazing furnace and shouted, "Shadrach, Meshach and Abednego, servants of the Most High God, come out! Come here!" So Shadrach, Meshach and Abednego came out of the fire, and the satraps, prefects, governors and royal advisers crowded around them. They saw that the fire had not harmed their bodies, nor was a hair of their heads singed; their robes were not scorched, there was no smell of fire on them."* There was no smell of fire or smoke!

Let's sum this all up. First, you will go through the Refiners fire to prepare yourself for eternity. He needs to get rid of all that is not of Him in you! *This third I will bring into the fire; I will refine them like silver and test them like gold. They will call on my name and I will answer them; I will say, 'They are my people, and they will say, 'The Lord is our God.'* (Zechariah 13:9) Our heavenly Father loves you so much that He wants you to be all that you were called to be in Christ. If you are in the fire right now consider it a high honor. There is no way that you can achieve the glory of all that you are called to be without the purifying stage! *As a prisoner for the Lord, then I urge you to live a life worthy of the calling you have received.* (Ephesians 4:1) Let me remind you that no one escapes this process and the process is never truly finished. We will be refined until the day He returns.

Second, Jesus will be there to hold you up! You can lean on Him as He carries you through! He wants you to endure! Don't forget, it is far better to be in the wilderness with Jesus than in the Promised Land without Him. *And the God of all grace, who called you to his eternal glory in Christ, after you have suffered a little while, will himself restore you and make you strong, firm and steadfast.* (1 Peter 5:10)

Lastly, once you come out of the fire you will not smell of smoke or fire but you will **be** more like Jesus! *Dear friends, now we are children of God, and what we will be has not yet been made known. But we know that when he appears, we shall be like him, for we shall see him as he is. Everyone who has this hope in him purifies himself, just as he is pure.* (1 John 3:2-3) That's living for an eternal purpose!

Let me be very clear and to the point with you right now. Do you mind? Listen up! God, your heavenly Father will never allow you to go through anything that He will not redeem. Let's put it into a measurement. Assume that the burden you are carrying weighs 100 pounds. If you are fully surrendering that burden to your Lord and Savior by allowing Him to carry it and work it out for His glory, the eternal reward will weigh at least 1,000 pounds! His power and strength increases your ability to carry an even greater burden for His glory. Read 2 Corinthians 4:17 with me. *For the light and momentary troubles are achieving for us an eternal glory that far outweighs them all.*

Toe Tapping

Do you understand what God is saying? He will redeem your obedience in trusting Him! That is why in Romans Paul calls us a " living sacrifice," because we can crawl back off the altar and say, " Hey, this is too much for me. I am out of here!" Everything is at stake if you crawl off and leave. Don't do it! Jesus has told us that His burdens are light. That is in comparison to the eternal value placed on the outcome! Stay in the fire with Jesus, it's only momentary compared to the eternal glory.

My lover spoke and said to me, "Arise, my darling, my beautiful one, and come with me. See! The winter is past; the rains are over and gone. Flowers appear on the earth; the season of singing has come, the cooing of doves is heard in our land." (Song of Solomon 2:11-12) If you persevere even when it feels hopeless and miserable you will eventually be brought out of that winter season and into spring and summer. That is where your joy becomes a toe tapping, birds singing, flower smelling, doves cooing joy! You don't want to miss out on that do you? You need to be so confident that God will bring you through the fire victoriously that the next time you are lying flat before the throne your feet start moving. Your eyes may be pouring tears, but your toes are tapping!

Shaking

We are in the final preparation stages for the return of Jesus right now. Meaning that His bride has to be ready! God's love for you is going to be arranging your preparation. In other words, there is going to be a "whole lot of shaking going on" in you. You need to read this next verse very carefully. *See to it that you do not refuse him who speaks.*

If they did not escape when they refused him who warned them on earth, how much less will we, if we turn away from him who warns us from heaven? At that time his voice shook the earth, but now he has promised, "Once more I will shake not only the earth but also the heavens." The words "once more" indicate the removing of what can be shaken-that is, created things- so that what cannot be shaken may remain. (Hebrews 12:25-27) God is in the business right now of shaking everything in you that is not of Him.

I pray veils have been lifted from your eyes during the course of this book. I pray that your walk with God is stronger and more powerful so that you endure the shaking. I pray that you are yielding and submitting to His will for your life with love overflowing in your heart.

The Prepared Bride

Let's read again the Parable of the Ten Virgins from Matthew 25:1-13:

> *At that time the kingdom of heaven will be like ten virgins who took their lamps and went out to meet the bridegroom. Five of them were foolish and five were wise. The foolish ones took their lamps but did not take any oil with them. The wise, however, took oil in jars along with their lamps. The bridegroom was a long time coming, and they all became drowsy and fell asleep.*
>
> *At midnight the cry rang out: "Here's the bridegroom! Come out to meet him!"*
>
> *Then all the virgins woke up and trimmed their lamps. The foolish ones said to the wise, "Give us some of your oil: our lamps are going out."*

No, they replied, "there may not be enough for both of us and you. Instead, go to those who sell oil and buy some for yourselves."

But while they were on their way to buy the oil, the bridegroom arrived. The virgins who were ready went in with him to the wedding banquet. And the door was shut.

Later the others also came, "Sir! Sir!" they said. "open the door for us!"

But he replied, "I tell you the truth, I don't know you."

Therefore, keep watch, because you so not know the day or the hour.

Prepare yourself as His holy bride. Think how you would feel if you were caught unprepared. It is absolutely the time to get ready for His imminent return. Don't miss the last dance.

Preparing for Him

Come, I will show you the bride, the wife of the Lamb.
(Revelation 21:9)

Prepare yourself for Jesus by understanding who you are in Him! You are a daughter of the King! You need to stand firm in the grace, love, mercy and power of your Father. That enables you to confidently take your position in the course of preparing for the Son. I have summed up for you what we have learned from this book to become more intimate with the Father and prepare yourself for an eternity with Jesus!

God is working to mature and perfect you. You do not want to miss out on the preparation stage. You will know the results are from Him. The fruit in your life from this process will be amazing. You will be amazing. The following are ways to prepare for His return. Let me emphasize here that these are spiritual activities that we are to strive for. We will never truly be complete until we are in His presence. An overcomer is one who is still in the race when He returns. You finish the race by just being in it.

- Live in the freedom Christ has purchased for you!
- Surrender with absolute trust to the Refiner's fire and look forward to the fruits and attributes of Jesus!
- Live victoriously in the power of His grace, love, and mercy!
- Yield to His will and character as the Spirit weaves His life into you!
- Drink of the Living Water and saturate yourself with His holy word.
- Pray without ceasing! Earnestly seek His face every day.
- Serve the body of Christ as He leads. Christ's bride is a servant!
- Live under the power of the blood and hold fast to His truths.
- Be willing to be a vessel to be used in any capacity God calls you!
- Dwell in the presence of perfect peace through shared sufferings with Christ.
- Be patient and long-suffering by enduring for His name.
- Become a witness to all people.
- Rejoice and give thanks always! Be joyful and praise His holy name in all things.
- Walk in a manner worthy of your call!
- Pray for all veils to be lifted from your face as you seek His wisdom and guidance.

- Live in a spirit of forgiveness and mercy, just as Christ has forgiven you!
- Never, ever look behind. Live in the moment focusing totally on Jesus!
- Obey His commands and promptings.
- Walk and leap in faith.
- Do not walk with the world. Rest intimately in the arms of Jesus!
- Know the truth and live it! I'll say it again, live the truth!
- Strive to overcome your flesh and live in the abundance of Him.
- Let Him dig your old self out and fill in the Living Water.
- Love the Lord Jesus with all your heart, soul and mind. Make Jesus your passion!
- Let go of any hindrances in your life that may be preventing the flow of God's power and glory!
- Know and trust His plan for your life.
- Love Him with submission and obedience.
- Dream and Dream Big! His dreams always come true!
- Be prepared and watching for Him.
- Last but not least, dance, you are the bride of Jesus!

So, my friends, how do you become a prepared bride for Jesus? You love Him. You simply love Him. (Matthew 22:37-38) He does all the rest. Your heavenly Bridegroom awaits your heart and your hand. Dance on!

Chapter Ten Study Questions

Before you begin pray for the wisdom and discernment needed to study His Holy Word!

Read Philippians 3:12-14 and write out verse 14.

I press toward the goal for the prize of the upward call of God.

Have any of is been made perfect? (Verse 12)

NO

What did Paul say to forget? (Verse 13)

those things which are behind.

Read with me verses 20-21 in Philippians 3. *But our citizenship is in heaven. And we eagerly await a Savior from there, the Lord Jesus Chris, who by the power that enables him to bring everything under his control, will transform our lowly bodies so that they will be like his glorious body.*

We will be perfect one day! Don't look behind. Look forward to that day!

Read 1 Corinthians 9:24-25 and fill in the blanks.

Do you not know that in a race all the runners run, but only one gets the prize? Everyone who competes in the games goes into __________ __________. They do it to get a __prize__ that will __not__ last; but we do it to get a __prize__ that __will__ last __forever__.

Whatever you are going through to possess an eternal crown will be worth it!

Write out and read aloud John 6:63. What does that verse say to you? the Spirit gives life

Spirit=Life: Flesh=Nothing.

Read James 1:2-16 and fill in the blanks:
(Verse 2)
Consider it pure joy, my brothers, whenever you face trials of many kinds, because you know that the testing of your faith develops patience. Perseverance must finish its work so that you may be perfect and complete, not lacking anything.

Did you notice the last part…we will not lack anything!

(Verse12)
Blessed is the man who endures under temptation, because when he has received the crown, he will receive the crown of life that God has promised to those who love Him.

Persevere for the eternal purpose you were called!

Read 2 Peter 1:3-11. And answer the following questions.

What has His divine power given us? (Verse 3)

all things - divine power

Why did God give us His precious promises? (Verse4)

divine nature

We should make every effort to add to our faith the following: goodness, knowledge, self-control, perseverance, godliness, brotherly kindness and love. These are some of attributes of a holy bride. How do you feel about that?

What does verse 8 say is the reason we should possess these qualities in *increasing measure*?

to be fruitful

Write out verse 10-11.

be more diligent —

A rich welcome would be nice!

Let's look at some of other attributes of Jesus. Read Philippians 2:1-17.

We see in these verses that Jesus did the following:

1. Emptied Himself
2. Took the nature of a servant
3. Humbled Himself
4. Became obedient unto death

Again, qualities of a holy bride! He is after a bride identical to Him! How did you feel about that list?

Now we can see what response God had towards Jesus' obedience.

1. God exalted him to the highest place.
2. God gave Him the name above every name.
3. God gave Him the authority so that knees bow and tongues confess that He is Lord.
4. God gave Him the glory and honor.

This is your Bridegroom!

Read 1 Corinthians 2:9 with me. *No eye has seen, no ear has heard, no mind has conceived what God has prepared for those who love him.*

Now read 2 Corinthians 4:18. *So we fix our eyes not on what is seen, but on what is unseen. For what is seen is temporary, but what is unseen is eternal.*

Write out 2 Corinthians 3:18. What happen when we portray unveiled faces?

We are transformed into His image

Write out 1 Thessalonians 5:23-24.

God of Peace - sanctifies us

Read Philippians 1:6 with me. *Being confident of this, that he who began a good work in you will carry it on to completion until the day of Christ Jesus.*

He will do it!

Write out Jeremiah 31:4. When the Lord rebuilds you what will you do?

rejoice

Write out Revelation 3:21.

sit by The Father

Read Revelation 22:17.

He who testifies to these things says, "Yes, I am coming soon." Amen. Come, Lord Jesus. (Revelation 22:20)

Let me pray Colossians 1: 9-12 over you my friend.

For this reason, since the day we heard about you, we have not stopped praying for you and asking God to fill you with the knowledge of his will through all spiritual wisdom and understanding. We pray this in order that you may live a life worthy of the Lord and may please him in every way: bearing fruit in every good work, growing in the knowledge of God, being strengthened with all power according to his glorious might so that you may have great endurance and patience, and joyfully giving thanks to the Father, who has qualified you to share in the inheritance of the saints in the kingdom of light.

In Jesus Name I Pray,
Amen.

Dance away!

Footprints With A Twist

Imagine you and the Lord Jesus
walking down the road together.
For much of the way, the Lord's footprints go along
steadily, consistently, rarely varying the pace.
But your footprints are a disorganized stream
of zigzags, starts, stops, turnarounds,
circles, departures and returns.
For much of the way, it seems to go like this,
but gradually your footprints come more in line
with the Lord's, soon parallelling His consistently.
You and Jesus are walking as true friends!

This seems perfect,
but then an interesting thing happens
your footprints, that once etched the sand next to Jesus',
are now walking precisely in His steps.
Inside His larger footprints
are your smaller ones,
showing that you and Jesus are becoming one.

This goes on for many miles,
but gradually you notice another change.
The footprints seem to grow larger.
Eventually, they disappear altogether.
There is only one set of footprints;
they have become one.

This goes on for a long time,
but suddenly the second set of footprints is back.
This time it seems even worse!
Zigzags all over the place.
Stops. Starts. Deeps gashes in the sand.
A veritable mess of prints.

You are amazed and shocked as your dream ends.
Now you pray: "Lord, I understand the first scene
with the zigzags and fits.
I was a new Christian; I was just learning.
But you walked on through the storm
and helped me learn to walk with you."
"That is correct," says Jesus.
"And when the smaller footprints were inside of Yours,
I was actually learning to walk in Your steps;
I followed you very closely."
"Very good. You understand everything so far,"
confirms the Lord.
"When the smaller footprints grew and filled in Yours,
I supposed that I was becoming like you in every way."
"Precisely."
"So, Lord, was there a regression or something?
The footprints separated,
and this time it was worse than at first."

There is a pause as the Lord
answers with a smile in His voice.
"You didn't know? That was when we danced!"

Author Unknown

There is a time for everything,
and a season for every activity under heaven:
a time to weep and a time to laugh,
and a time to mourn
and a time to dance.
(Ecclesiastes 3:1,4,9)

Bibliography

Booker, Richard. *Here Comes the Bride*. (Houston, Texas: Sounds of the Trumpet, 1995.)

Lash, Jamie. *The Ancient Jewish Wedding*. (Ft. Lauderdale, Florida: Jewish Jewels, 1997.)

Routtenberg, Lilly S. and Seldin, Ruth R. *The Jewish Wedding Book*. (New York, N.Y.: Harper & Row, Publishers, Inc., 1967.)

Vine, W.E., Unger, Merrill F., and White, Jr., William. *Vine's Complete Expository Dictionary of Old and New Testament Words*. (Nashville, Tennessee: Thomas Nelson Publishers, 1984.)

Order Form

Postal orders:
ACW Press, 5501 N. 7th Ave., #502, Phoenix, AZ 85013

Telephone orders: (800) 931-BOOK (2665)

Please send *Dancing With Daddy to*:

Name:______________________________________

Address:_____________________________________

City:________________________ State:_____

Zip:_________

Telephone: (____) ____________

Book Price: $10.00 in U.S. dollars.

Shipping: $4.00 for the first book and $1.00 for each additional book to cover shipping and handling within US, Canada, and Mexico. International orders add $7.00 for the first book and $3.00 for each additional book.